STANDING STRONG

STANDING STRONG

Jennie Morton

For more information e-mail StandingStrong.Jennie@yahoo.com

Book design by:
Arbor Books, Inc.
www.arborbooks.com
Printed in the United States of America

Standing Strong
Jennie Morton

1. Title 2. Author 3. Memoir

Library of Congress Control Number: 2012922114
ISBN: 978-0-615-73069-1

Dedicated to my four children, Kylan, Kaytlin, Aidan, and Hunter: I love you with all my heart and all of who I am. You shall always know the love of this mom—YOUR MOM—is so much more than anyone ever could have imagined. I went to the end of the world and back for you, walked through fire and survived. I never stopped loving, thinking of, and fighting for you and our family. I hope you read this and know how strongly I love you and how I would do anything for all of you. Neither money nor power could quash my love or make me go away. Never in a million years would I have thought your tiny bodies would have to deal with so much and endure such devastation. For that I am truly sorry. I want you to know it was never my intention. I never meant to pull you into this battle scarred with ill intent. You were always at the forefront of my mind, and I wish peace, prosperity, and happiness for you.

Your MOM learned many things upon this twisting road called life, and with this came my heartfelt reason for being—my destiny. My voice and my friends' voices became the voices for children across the nation and the world. Even though people do things without thinking of their lasting effects, I want you to understand that you deserve both your mother and father. When the time comes, I hope you can find that part of me that lies within you and forgive your fathers and the system for what they have done.

May you always know you are the best choices I ever made and the most important parts of my life.

Love always,
MOM

CHAPTER 1

The Long and Winding Road

How did I get here?

It was Friday afternoon and the air conditioner in my car blew out crisp, cool air. I'd just gotten it fixed, and it was a relief to feel those icy bursts of air once again. There was no relief to be found in Texas's summer nights and I'd be in the car a long time. I was about to start the first half of my eight-hour drive for the day. I'd be back doing this again on Sunday afternoon, but I tried not to think about that. I hated it, but I didn't have a choice. It was the only way I'd get to see my precious boys, Aidan and Hunter, and I wouldn't miss out on that treasured time for anything in the world.

My mom came out of the house clutching the latest Danielle Steel in one hand and a tumbler of iced tea for the road in the other. We'd talk for a few minutes before she'd crack the spine on her book, eager to get in a little bit of reading before the sun went down for the night.

As she buckled up and I started the car, we gave each other weary smiles and settled in for the long drive.

As I navigated Dallas's heavy Friday afternoon traffic, inching my way to I-45, I asked myself again how the sharp left turns of my life had led me to this point. If you would have told me a year ago that I'd be here, I would have laughed and told you that you were crazy.

And yet, here I was.

The year before, I'd been a busy mom, with all my children living under one roof. It was a hectic life with lots of hugs and kisses; many days I didn't know if I was coming or going, and I loved every minute of it. My children had everything they needed and more: the best clothes, a big, beautiful home in an exclusive Houston suburb, and a ton of activities to stimulate their minds and bodies. I had an awesome job as a pharmaceutical sales representative that I loved, where I ranked number one in the nation and had graced the stage on multiple occasions to accept award in recognition of my achievements.

Most importantly, my children had me whenever they needed me, twenty-four hours a day.

Now, a year later, my dream world had turned into a horrible nightmare. I'd always been an overachiever, and consider myself to be a good person with a big heart. All of those positive qualities were turned against me and used to bring me to my knees. During the past year, I'd shelled out close to $200,000 in attorney's fees, lost my job because I spent more time in court than at work, been bullied from the town I'd lived in for twelve years, and suffered unimaginable psychological abuse at the hands of my tormentor, who'd promised me more than once, "I'll break you."

I'd grown up believing justice would always prevail. However, if there's anything this journey has taught me it is that the system is corrupt and can be twisted around your neck until it chokes the life out of you. I'd expected that law enforcement, the district attorney, and the court system were there to protect us. However, these officials who'd been sworn to uphold the law and protect me and my family were as shady as a tree-lined street.

My tormentor came from a wealthy, powerful, highly connected family, and each and every one of them would go to any lengths necessary to harm me and those around me. My friends were harassed, and their lives were threatened. After I was remarried, my new husband lost two jobs and was assaulted twice by my tormentor. And yet the police did nothing. I spent more time documenting what was happening in my life than I did living it. I tried in vain to get protective orders, made countless 911 calls, and pressed harassment charges. I even went to the DA in tears, begging for help. Time and again I was turned away and told I would need to go through the court system.

However, the court system betrayed me. Law enforcement would not protect me. My tormentor was given an open ticket to abuse me without repercussion. The system turned its back on me because my tormentor had influence and connections I could never hope to have. After all my efforts to protect my family, I lost my two boys due to the unethical and illegal acts of many.

I shifted in my seat as traffic on I-45 broke open, and I was able to pick up speed. I looked over at my mom, engrossed in her book, turning the pages fast. The court had mandated that if I wanted to see my little boys, my mom would have to accompany me on that long stretch of road between Dallas and Houston—just one more turn of the knife inside me.

I don't share my story with you to make you feel sorry for me. This is meant to be a story of inspiration to others who have loved and lost. This is for women *and* men dealing with custody issues while trying to maintain a sound family structure. I tell you about the things that have happened to me to give you hope. So many of us lose our optimism and believe we should remain shrouded in darkness, with no way of ever finding our way out into the light. The depths of our despair are oftentimes so deep we wish the tide would just take us.

No one should ever, *ever* feel like there's nothing left to fight for, no matter how bad it gets.

What I've gone through in my life would have broken most, which was the intent of my tormentor. However, I made the conscious decision to keep going. I will never curl up in a little ball and die. I will never stop fighting to get my kids back. I will never let my tormenter beat me. I will keep getting back up.

I will stand strong.

CHAPTER 2

How It All Began

When you reach a crossroads in life, it usually makes you want to look back so you can try to trace how you got there. You hope that somehow your past will provide the answers to help you figure out how you got to where you are in the present. The most important thing to remember, though, is that you've got to learn from the past so you won't continue to make those same mistakes in the future.

Looking back on my own life, I can see that my strong desire for a family has really been at the heart of everything I've done in my personal life. Family means everything to me, and all I ever wanted was a strong marriage to a loving husband, with a house full of kids around us. It was that pursuit of a loving and happy home that led me into four marriages, all before I was thirty-five. Though each of my marriages ended in divorce, three of them resulted in my beautiful children, so I can't consider them failures.

As I've gotten older, I've begun to understand the power of intuition and the great gifts it can bring to our lives if we'll only stop and take the time to listen. It comes in many forms. It may be a strong physical sensation; it could be a dream; it could be a voice that begins as a whisper and swells to a mighty roar. Whatever it is, it lives in all of us, but so many of us choose to brush it aside and lead with what we *choose* to see rather than what we *should* see. I've been so guilty of this in my life, and I've paid dearly for it. Had I been tuned in to my own voice, my own wisdom, my own gut feelings, I would have seen what was staring me in the face all along, and thus made better choices. The cold hard truth I've had to face in my life is that not everyone wishes you well. I consider myself to be a good person—always have—and because of that I strive to see only the good in those around me, not their true selves. I put my own wants and desires ahead of fact, and, along with many of the lessons I've learned on my journey, I've had to realign my vision of the world and those in it. Did wanting to see the best in people blind me to red flags and lead me down some wrong paths? I can say with absolute clarity that yes, it did. But as that old spiritual says, wouldn't take nothin' for my journey now. While I've walked through the fire, and have the scars and burns to show for it, I don't regret anything in my life. All I can do now is take the gifts of what I've learned from my past and use them to make a better future for myself and my kids.

When I turn the telescope to look backward in time, I can see so clearly where the seeds of my future were sown. While I have always excelled at everything I've put my mind to, there has always been a tiny piece of me that has felt as though I live under a bad sign, as though a dark and stormy cloud hovers above my head and at any moment can rain down on me, leaving a series of catastrophes in its wake. I trace this feeling back to traumas I suffered in childhood—ones I never realized I had been carrying around with me like a great big anchor affixed to my neck. They had been weighing me down for much of my adult life. So many of us never realize how childhood can impact us in the future. We falsely believe that once we grow up, we leave our childhoods behind and they don't shape who we eventually become. That couldn't be further from the truth. Every experience, every emotion—sad, happy, funny, disappointing—lays an unmistakable foundation for our adult lives. Like anything in life, it's what we choose to do with this information that can direct the path we follow.

As children much of our self-worth is derived from our parents and the way in which they interact with us. This is often why one of the first things you are asked about in therapy is what your childhood was like. When you grow up feeling as though you never got the love and approval of your parents, you'll seek it out in other, sometimes inappropriate places. This can and will wreak havoc in your life later on down the road. Parenting is the hardest job there is, and if you don't give it your full attention, or if you treat it in a cavalier fashion, the consequences can be devastating for the child.

My childhood had a tumultuous beginning; the problems actually go back to before I was even born. People often told me that when they looked at me they saw a beautiful woman with the world on a string—I had a successful career, a beautiful home, nice clothes, and cars. Many people assumed I'd been given all these luxuries, which wasn't true. I was not so lucky as to have everything good in my life handed to me. I worked extremely hard and overcame a lot of adversity to achieve everything I have. I started behind the eight ball because I didn't have the support of my family. In fact for many years my mother and I had a strained relationship, and if anything our difficulties drove me to become a success.

My mother comes from a large family, and in looking back I am reminded of the saying that those who ignore history are doomed to repeat it. Much of my personal history would come to parallel my mother's many years later. She was the oldest of six children, and eventually each of her siblings was taken from my grandmother. Her father, my grandfather, was a Navy man, and thus had a hard life. He turned to alcohol for a respite from his demons, and he often went on violent drinking binges, several of which landed him in jail.

During this time, his wife, my grandmother, was brutally raped. She was desperate to keep her six children with her, but it was like trying to keep a lid on a pressure cooker that's about to blow. She didn't have the financial or emotional resources to look after six spirited children. To help make ends meet, she began to write hot checks all over town in order to keep the children clothed and fed. Once my grandfather, who'd been released from prison, found out, he stepped in and took the blame for her crimes. He reasoned that his wife was in the precarious situation she was in because he hadn't been there for her in her time of need. He felt he was more equipped to cope with being in jail than she was, so he sacrificed himself to save her.

The trauma was too much for my grandmother. Her husband was in jail to protect her, she was attempting to care for six children, and she was still healing from the sexual assault. She succumbed to a nervous breakdown. It was my mother's call to the authorities that placed my grandmother in the hospital for treatment.

Her mother's departure meant the care and feeding of her five brothers and sisters fell on my mom's slender, twelve-year-old shoulders. She took on the role of caretaker for the family, hiding the dire circumstances from the outside world. Eventually the State of Louisiana discovered the situation and went about separating the siblings, placing them with an aunt and uncle. My mother, along with two of her siblings, was placed in the same foster home, though they would be separated many times over the years. The other three children were sent to another foster home, later to be adopted.

We discovered later that the aunt and uncle who'd taken the family in had contacted the State of Louisiana to come and take the children away. They had a family of six themselves, and it was overwhelming now to be responsible for

twelve children. Financially they just could not bear that
burden, and in their minds the only solution was for the kids
to be turned over to the state.

As you can imagine, this had a devastating impact on my
mother. She felt responsible for the breakup of the family, as
though somehow she had failed her brothers and sisters as
well as her mother. She was extremely bitter about this turn
of events for years and grew a major chip on her shoulder.
Her way of dealing with these multiple losses was to harden
herself to them and act as if they didn't exist. It was the only
way she knew how to handle her grief and tremendous sense
of loss.

Once my grandmother was released from the hospital, she
tried in vain to find her children. Although she hit numerous
dead ends, she never gave up trying to get all her children
back. Her relationship with my mother would continue
to be complicated. My mother never had a stable mother
figure in her life, which would impact how she interacted
with me. Many years later, when she was older, my mother
would mend fences with her mother, and the relationship
would blossom, but for most of her life she held bitterness
and resentment toward her, blaming her in part for what had
happened. However, it was my mother who held the heaviest
burden for the decimation of the family.

A desire to change her circumstances led my mother to
marry my father at the tender age of sixteen and move to
Texas; my birth followed later that year, and my sister came
along two years after me. Although my mother had tried to

keep her own family together when she was a little girl, in truth she wasn't prepared for the responsibility of being a young wife and mother. As I said, she'd never had a stable mother figure, so a vital anchor was missing in her life. She had no one to turn to for guidance.

My father did shift work, so he often wasn't home, leaving my mother alone to try to figure out how to navigate things on her own. However, she didn't have the commitment that was required. She wanted to do all the typical things a teenage girl does, like hang out with her friends and go to parties. She fell in with the wrong crowd, which resulted in a fractured relationship between us that would last for decades.

When I was two and a half years old, my grandmother had managed to reunite some of the family, which stirred a deep longing in my mother. Her sister, Susie, and brother, Tommy, had been found and were back with my grandmother in Louisiana. Missing her long-lost siblings, and unhappy in her marriage to my father, my mother took my sister and me and fled to Louisiana.

The two years I was away from my father and under the care of my mother played a major role in shaping the adult I became. Although I was two and a half during that time, my memories of that era in my life are crystal clear. People always ask me how I can remember things from when I was so little. For one I've always had a stellar memory, and second, the things that happened during that era were stamped onto me. I couldn't forget them even if I tried.

We lived in a rundown trailer with no front or side

doors, meaning anyone could come in at any time of the day or night. I can remember my mother's boyfriends being around during that time, the frequent use of alcohol, hearing fragments of drug names like "black mollies" and "acid," and seeing people shoot up. There was another man I have memories of looking at and being scared of because of the way his eyes rolled to the back of his head and the beads of sweat on his forehead. Just as I asked my mother what was wrong with him, he threw up all over me. For many years after that incident I had an extreme phobia about vomit. If someone next to me was throwing up I would be hit with my own wave of nausea and break out in perspiration. When I got older, I thought about pursuing a medical career, but the idea of people vomiting around me all the time was enough to staunch that thought. I could handle blood and bodily fluids, but not that. It wasn't until I had babies that I was able to retrain my brain about it. Babies throw up all the time, and I certainly couldn't run away from them when they got sick!

Admittedly, my mother was wrapped up in her own life during this time and wasn't thinking clearly about the care of her two young daughters. To this day I don't know where she went, but she left us in a motel room once for two days with no food. My poor baby sister screamed and cried from hunger, and the only thing I knew to do was fill her bottle with water. I climbed my two-and-a-half-year-old body onto the countertop of the bathroom and put water from the sink into her bottle. It would calm her for a little while, but it wasn't long before her screams of hunger would begin again. I too would try to sustain myself on water, but the most vivid memory I have is leaning over the back of a chair to distract myself from the growls and protests of my empty stomach. Strings of saliva hung out of my mouth as I waited for something, anything, to happen.

Were it not for housekeeping coming in to clean the room on that second day, I'm fairly certain it wouldn't have been long before we starved to death. I didn't know enough to tell them where my mother was or how she could be reached. I was able to tell them about my aunt Sue Sue (my mother's younger sister, Susie) and that my grandmother, whom I am named for, had the last name Campbell. Miraculously the motel staff was able to find them, and my sister and I were whisked away to stay with my grandmother and Sue Sue, who I considered to be like a mom.

There were uglier episodes to follow that particular incident. Some traumas leave a permanent imprint on your brain. I have memories of seeing a man blow his face off during a game of Russian roulette; my mother was in the bathroom, and this man repeatedly put this gun to his head: *click, click, click.* Though I was young, I knew something was not right with this situation. The gun discharged, and the bullet ricocheted straight through the wall behind him and into the bathroom, where my mother was sitting on the toilet. The bullet missed her but took out a chunk of wall right above her head. She darted out of the bathroom, scooped up my sister and me, and ran out the back door. There were no steps to the ground, so we fell a few feet down into the grass and broken twigs. She yelled at us to run, screaming that the police would come and take us away from her. Stickers pierced the bottoms of my little feet as we scurried through those woods. Tears streamed down my face because my feet hurt so much, but my mother kept pushing us to keep going, knowing if we stopped it would be all over.

My mother was warned by her mother that she needed to get her act together. She tried to provoke a response by reaching into the painful past and bringing it into the present, asking my mother if she wanted her children taken away as her own children had been ripped from her. It was a valiant effort on my grandmother's part, but the words didn't have the intended effect. As anyone knows, change begins with the individual. You have to want to take steps in your life to change your behavior, and it doesn't matter how much reinforcement you get from others; if you're not ready to walk that path, you will stay stuck running down the same road.

My father even stepped in and told my mother he would take us away from her if she didn't stop putting us at risk. It was unheard of in the '70s for a father to be granted full custody of his children no matter how dire the circumstances. Nevertheless, he consulted a lawyer and was told that because we were in another state he'd have to find an attorney in Louisiana, and secondly it would be quite tough to produce tangible evidence that we were in eminent danger under my mother's care. While he still came to see us each weekend, he felt as though pursuing a custody action against my mother would be futile. He wasn't willing to subject us to such a harrowing ordeal.

In spite of all the emotional and physical turmoil being with my mother brought me, there was nothing in me that wanted to be separated from her. Regardless of her mistakes or the ways she might have let me down, she was still my mom, and I wanted to be with her. There is nothing that can break the bond between a mother and a child. No matter the ups and downs and turbulent twists and turns, the bond goes beyond the physical; it is an emotional and spiritual tie that, no matter how much you try to outrun it or deny its existence, it is always there for you.

During our two-year odyssey in Louisiana, I turned three years old, and my world was forever changed when I was subjected to a brutality no child should ever have to endure. It was nighttime, and my sister, who was about a year old, lay sleeping in the bed next to me in the trailer with no front or side doors; my mother was in the other room. I heard noises in our room and woke up to see a man standing over the bed. He instructed me to take off my underwear. Although I was just a little girl, I knew what he was asking me to do wasn't right. I shook my head no, hoping he would go away. Besides being afraid of what he might do to me, I was terrified my sister would wake up and he would hurt us both.

He moved closer and grabbed my leg, telling me if I didn't take off my underwear he would cut them off. It was only when he pulled out a knife and showed it to me that I believed he would. I can still remember the blade shimmering in the moonlight as he waved it around, sending flashes of light all around the room. Still I refused to comply with his request.

The last thing I remember is my underwear being sliced off my body. I've blacked out what happened, though my counselors tell me I know exactly what that man did to me that night. Even more frightening was that he wasn't a random stranger who just happened upon our trailer; I recognized him as one of my mother's friends and someone who had been in the trailer many times over the past year. During his assault on me, my sister woke up and started to cry. He fled, and I tried my best to comfort her and dry her tears.

After I got her back to sleep, all I wanted was my mom. I ran out to wake her and tell her about the man in my room and what he had done. She told me I was dreaming, and to go back to bed. No matter how insistent I was that there had been a man in my room, she was just as adamant that I'd dreamt the whole thing, and ordered me to go back to sleep. The shreds of my underwear hung from my fingers. I implored her to please look at what this man had done to my underwear. My pleas for comfort, and more importantly for belief that what I was saying was true, went unheard as my mother told me once and for all to go back to bed. I cried myself to sleep that night, scared because of what had happened to me and sad that my mother didn't believe any of it.

The assault happened around Christmastime, and I can remember crawling into my mother's lap the next morning, looking at all the decorations but feeling far from celebratory.

My little body shook with tears as I told my mother how much it hurt my feelings that she didn't believe what I had told her, that I felt like she didn't care about me. When I told her I knew who the man was and gave her his name, she shushed me, warning me not to say another word. Years later I found out she had told my uncle Tommy what had happened, and he had tracked this man down and pulverized him, knocking every one of his teeth loose from his mouth. At the time, however, my mother's repeated admonitions to be quiet, to not say anything, spoke volumes to me; in my mind she was condoning what this monster had done to me by insisting we sweep it under the rug and keep everything quiet. After that I never quite trusted her to have my well-being at heart, and it was at that point our emotional estrangement began. I needed a mother.

When I think about the inherent differences between my mother's personality and my own, I think of it as a balloon. If you fill up a balloon with air, it has no choice but to burst wide open. That's the way I am; if I don't let out whatever is bothering me, I will explode all over the place, but once I've expressed my feelings I can move past whatever was on my mind. My mother, however, will keep everything inside. Her balloon may swell to capacity, but it will never blow up; the air will seep out and the balloon will recede down to a silent, little shell.

I remained angry at her for not taking action, while she—knowing she had failed me—was mad at me because I served as a constant reminder that she had not done right by her own daughter. I know now that my mother's reaction was one of fear and shock and helplessness. She didn't know how to process what had happened to me and didn't know how to help me. We were at an impasse, a horrible logjam neither of us could get past. We would have numerous emotional confrontations about the situation many times over the years, each one of us receding from the battle more bruised than ever.

It wasn't until I was in my twenties and turned it over to God that I was able to let go of the hurt, bitterness, and resentment. What had happened happened, and I would never know why that man had cut off my underwear in the dead of night. I finally let it go and forgave my mother.

Last year she pulled me aside and told me she felt there was something I needed to hear from her. She apologized profusely for what had happened that night and for what had happened after, taking full responsibility for not showing me the compassion and understanding I so desperately needed that night. Although I had long ago moved past the hurt and betrayal, it still unleashed a flood of tears. All I'd wanted for thirty-seven years was an acknowledgement and apology from my mother. I was so overcome with love and emotion the only thing I could do was hug my mother's neck and let her know she'd been long forgiven in my heart. While it took many years and travel over many difficult paths, we finally arrived at a destination of peace, love, and, most importantly, respect in our relationship.

Not long after that incident we went home to Texas and

my father. Despite a two-year separation, my parents never got a divorce, though they each dated others during that time. In fact my father had more than moved on, becoming involved in a serious relationship with a woman he planned to marry. Hearing my father's plans, coupled with what had happened to me, was a wake-up call for my mother. She realized what a good, stable man my father was, and the crowd she'd fallen in with had caused her nothing but trouble. She was ready to get off drugs and away from the bad influences, and put our family back together. These bonds were too strong for my parents to ignore, and they made the decision to resume their marriage. We were a family once more.

In tracing the path I've been on since birth, I've found I was a people pleaser, a good girl who was strong on the inside and ready to speak up about injustice and do the right thing, yet was told to be quiet because there were certain things you just didn't talk about. Many of my good-girl tendencies stem from my upbringing and the influence my parents exerted over every aspect of my life.

After we returned from Louisiana, my mother became a completely different person. Gone was the hard-partying woman who didn't want to be tied down by a husband and family; in her place appeared a hard-working woman dedicated to her kids, one who would live by the letter of the law. She and my father renewed their vows, and there was never again any talk of drugs or alcohol. She restored her faith in God and began to attend church regularly. Much of my own drive and penchant for being an overachiever derives from her, as she became an entrepreneur, helming three or four successful businesses at a time and eventually becoming a degreed accountant. She was a highly efficient person, and she set extremely high standards for herself and for us. There was much about her I admired, but she was still a mystery to me.

It was only when I got older that I recognized the link between what had happened during the Louisiana years and my adolescence. My parents didn't want my sister and me to go down the same path my mother had with drugs and alcohol, and therefore they made it their mission to provide us with a stable home. However there were no easy rides, and they set the bar quite high for us. We led a disciplined existence, and, having seen what being out of control wrought, we didn't want to let our parents down and fall prey to those temptations. My parents were the first people I wanted to please, and I was terrified ever to disappoint them or go against any of the austere conventions laid down by them.

My little sister and I lived by a strict rule book that mandated we conduct ourselves like budding young ladies. We weren't allowed to call boys or spend endless hours on the phone with our friends, and being out on the weekends was not allowed. We could choose either Friday or Saturday night to spend time with friends, but never both. The rules of my household were strictly enforced, even when I was at a girlfriend's house. There would be phone calls to ensure I had not lied regarding my whereabouts, and I adhered to my 11:00 p.m. weekend curfew.

Most children feel as though their parents have eyes in the back of their heads, and I was no different. I grew up in the tiny town of Athens, Texas, and just as in most small towns everyone knew everybody else, and your misdeeds would surely make it back to your parents—so in a way my parents did indeed have eyes everywhere. Wherever I was I maintained proper decorum, and my determination to stay on the straight and narrow never wavered. School was no different; I maintained an A average, received scholarly awards, and participated in numerous extracurricular activities like track and baseball. While a part of me went out for sports and competition programs to satisfy my naturally competitive and outgoing nature, they also fulfilled an innate need in me to break free of the constraints my parents had fastened around my neck. How I enjoyed those little chunks of time every afternoon or during weekend meets in another town— those afterschool activities were an escape I cherished.

Since I grew up in the Bible Belt, church and religion were part of my bloodline. My parents kept us glued to the pews every Wednesday and Sunday with no exceptions; even if I spent the night with a friend, I was expected to be at church bright and early on Sunday morning.

I actually met my first husband, Dana, through church. He was introduced to me by my younger sister when I was fifteen and he was sixteen. He had sandy-blond hair and warm, brown eyes, and was as skinny as a toothpick. However he was sweet and extremely respectful of me, and was the first boy I ever really had the opportunity to be attracted to. We had some great conversations and shared many of the same likes and dislikes. Since I was so sheltered by my parents, by the time I met Dana I'd never been on a real date, never even kissed a boy romantically, so Dana was my first anything and everything. Since my graduating class only had thirty-two students and I'd grown up with all of them, I didn't have any interest in going on dates with any of them.

Due to the strict rules of my household, which dictated no movie or dinner dates until I was sixteen, Dana and I were bound to my house for our courtship, and it was during those long conversations in my living room under my parents' distant but watchful eyes that we began to plan our future. While a lot of people may think we were too young to be thinking so far ahead, in truth, for the small town we lived in, it wasn't that unusual to be talking about marriage at seventeen and eighteen years old. In fact the valedictorian and salutatorian of my class had both married and had babies by our senior year. Besides I had always considered myself an old soul and quite mature when compared to other teenagers my age. I worked all through high school and saved my money, and I had already taken some college courses at Texas Tech University to get a jump on my academics beyond high school. My hard work paid off, and I was awarded the Presidential Award of Academic Excellence, landing a scholarship in the process. I was more than ready to start building my dream of having a family.

I married Dana when I was seventeen years old, and, as you might expect, we experienced a multitude of ups and downs during our years together. Though we were both extremely responsible young adults, we still had our share of the trials and tribulations associated with being a young couple beginning their life together as husband and wife. Money was tight, even with us working three jobs between us. Neither one of us had lived on our own before, so we had a lot to learn not only about how to be married, but how to function in the world as conscientious members of society.

Our fortunes began to turn when the engine repair shop where Dana worked was put up for sale, and we decided to take a chance on his dream of being a business owner and bought it. We were so successful we opened up a second location, and within a year we'd gone from scraping by on three hundred dollars a week to generating more than one million dollars in revenue from both shops combined.

While I was grateful for the financial benefits we were beginning to reap in our lives, the greatest blessing arrived in the form of our beautiful boy, Kylan. Of all the heights I have scaled and successes I have known, becoming a mother was the most bountiful and treasured gift of my time on this earth. I felt as though God looked down and smiled as he bestowed on me this perfect little miracle. I was thrilled to be a mother and felt as though the dream I'd held since childhood had come to wonderful and glorious fruition.

Once I had a child of my own, I did what so many daughters do: I vowed I would not repeat the actions of my mother before me. While my early years with my mother were marked by recklessness, once I was older she over-compensated by exerting too much control over my life. In truth my sister and I probably should have been taken from my mother during the Louisiana years, but that was not the way the hand was played. Instead of becoming a nurturing person, she went too far in the other direction, which can also have consequences. I became a people pleaser—someone who spent too much time trying to keep the peace instead of standing up and fighting for myself when the time came.

With Kylan, and later my other three younger children, my instinct was to be protective of them, but I also made the conscious decision not to smother them in a controlling way, the way I had been treated for so much of my life. You can't watch over your children 24/7, nor can you bend them to your will without expecting a fallout of some kind down the line. I took the stance of being a mother to my children while encouraging their own natural personalities and talents to shine through. I taught them about making choices and the benefits and/or consequences of each choice they made. I wanted them to be their own people, not clones of me.

Kylan's birth brought me nothing but happiness, and from that day on I knew I was meant to be a mother. I held the belief nothing would pierce that cocoon of joy wrapped around me; I honestly thought Dana and I would go on that way until death did us part. The nail in the coffin of our marriage was the wedge that has split apart so many mar-riages—we grew up, and we grew apart. Neither Dana nor I had ever been ones to partake in excessive drinking or partying, so it was both stunning and hurtful to me when my husband turned to these pursuits. He was in the throes of a delayed adolescence, and it caused him to make poor decisions where our relationship and family unit were concerned. He began to betray the sanctity of our marriage and show me immense disrespect by staying away from home all night and even turning to hardcore drugs.

My husband forced me into the unenviable position of confronting his transgressions and the ongoing insolence he displayed toward me and our home. The situation between Dana and I became increasingly precarious and volatile as he unleashed his rage on me with stunning ferocity. These horrific episodes he perpetrated on me resulted in emotional abuse and debilitating damage to my person, including an incident where he hurled a burning log at me, causing me to nearly lose my sight permanently. I could not continue to put my life or the life of my child at risk, so, unbeknownst to him, I initiated the heartbreaking process of planning an exit strategy from my marriage. Once I'd made up my mind to leave, I did so with little fanfare, packing up my belongings while he was at work and closing the door on that chapter of my life. I was done, and there would be no turning back.

It is often during times of great upheaval and strife in our lives that we have to rely on something greater than ourselves to pull us through to the other side of the darkness. I called upon my faith, letting those principles that had been instilled in me from the day I was born guide me toward what I felt and knew was a greater existence for myself and my son. All too often far too many of us make the decision to stay in toxic or dangerous situations that are ultimately detrimental to our souls. We may feel sentimental about the people we've chosen as our mates; we convince ourselves being with someone who clearly does not hold us in the highest regard is better than being alone. We explain away vile, treacherous behavior with a multitude of justifications. So many of us are afraid to stand on our own two feet and use them to walk on to a more abundant life.

I personally got married to stay married; I did not go into my union with Dana thinking there would be an end-point. I got married for life, and it was that firmly held belief, coupled with the fact we shared a child, and my love for him that kept me there longer than I should have been. I would urge anyone who is in a situation where love and respect are not the ruling forces to expect more for themselves. It can be so hard to find that inner strength, but once you reach down deep inside you'll be amazed what lies at the core.

CHAPTER 3

Dreams Dashed

I look back on this time of my life as one of great transition and one in which my fortitude would be severely tested. It would have been easy for me to curl up in a little ball and hide in my own safe, little corner of the world feeling sorry for myself. But I couldn't; I had to pick myself up, dust myself off, and put one foot in front of the other to keep going.

In order to regroup and determine what the next steps of my life would be, I found myself once again under the watchful eye of my parents, as I had moved home. The adjustment was not an easy one for any of us, as my parents had a difficult time seeing me as anything but their little girl who had to be given curfews and told what to do and when to do it. I chafed under their stringent rules and reminded them what the truth of my situation was; I was a grown woman—a mother—who'd already lived a lifetime in just a few short years, and therefore the dictates I'd lived under during my childhood and adolescence no longer applied.

As I tried to navigate the rough waters of being an adult child living under my parents' roof, I turned my attention to other, more pressing matters, which was to finish my education, bringing me one step closer to my lifelong dream of a career as a lawyer. I held the legal profession in the highest esteem, believing it to be the pinnacle of affecting positive change in people's lives. The law is there to protect us from the known evils of the world; we are all entitled to due process and representatives of the legal system are sworn to uphold our rights. I've always been prone to helping those who are less fortunate, and to me becoming a lawyer would afford me the opportunity to do so. I was bound and determined to realize my dream no matter how hard the struggle.

I was in the midst of turning my dream into a reality when I met my second husband, Chuck. I was going to a community college in the Dallas area while he worked in Houston-Conroe as an engineer. Unlike Dana, who I'd met in church, Chuck and I met at a bar. While I was attracted to his dark, good looks, and slender frame, I was most smitten with his authenticity. He made his commitment clear to me without my having to prod him to do so. Once a week he would drive four hours to spend a few hours with me before making the return trip home. Not many men would make that type of sacrifice for a woman, and those actions on Chuck's part revealed much about his character, his values, and who he was at his core. These were attractive qualities to me, because it meant he wasn't just out for a fling, but truly wanted an honest and open relationship with me. I was deeply in love with him and thrilled when he asked me to marry him.

With my union with Chuck and the completion of my education, it felt as though the pieces of my life were falling into place one by one. I believe good things can happen in our lives and it is up to each and every one of us to be open to receive the bounty. If the door is locked when the delivery comes, we can't be surprised when we never get the package. Marrying Chuck and starting our lives together as man and wife was freshly tilled soil upon which my other lifelong dream could grow and flourish with abandon and joy. I would finally be getting the stable, loving family I'd always wanted.

I was married to Chuck for seven years, and most of it was filled with endless bliss and blessings. Our personalities and temperaments were perfectly meshed with each other, so much so that it was two years before we had our first fight as man and wife, a feat not many couples can claim. Our circle of joy only expanded when I gave birth to our daughter, Kaytlin. Much like when Kylan was born, Kaytlin's birth filled me with such purpose and passion. I'd always yearned for a little girl, and her arrival was yet another sign to me that I had lived my life with an open and loving heart, and was now being rewarded with another gift.

Chuck, Kaytlin, and I settled into an easy domesticity. I

stayed home with the baby while Chuck went to work. For a time this established routine worked well for our marriage and our family. However I couldn't let go of that long-held desire to strive for the other things I wanted out of life— namely a career as a lawyer. It was a calling, and I could not ignore the ringing of that message.

As Kaytlin grew into an energetic and cheerful toddler, I decided the time was right to pick up the mantle of education once more and resume my studies. I graduated summa cum laude with multiple honors, was named most outstanding psychology major, and was accepted into Southwest Texas School of Law. I couldn't have known it then, but law school would spell the end of my marriage to Chuck. It consumed much of my spare time and energy; it required endless amounts of reading and preparation and, given my natural tendency to excel at any task I take on, I knew it would not be enough just to read the material and show up for class. It was imperative that I understood the information and was able to recall it with confidence and an ability to analyze and apply it.

As time went on, Chuck became increasingly resentful of the time I spent on my studies. It became clear to me that he feared this new path I was on would carry me away from him and our life together. I saw it so differently; it would make me happy and therefore only enhance our partnership. However, once the roles in our home began to shift underneath our feet, Chuck became desperate to return to the status quo. He waged a relentless campaign to convince me to abandon my studies and refocus my attention on being the wife and mother I had been. His weapon of choice was unyielding badgering, and when that didn't work he issued an appalling ultimatum: I was to choose him and our marriage or law school, but I could not have both in my life. It was unacceptable to him that I continue on this journey.

I gave up a part of my soul the day I acquiesced and capitulated to Chuck's demands. With a heavy heart, I drafted my withdrawal letter, which Chuck helped me to craft. As I turned the letter over to my professors, little fragments of me shattered inside; all my hopes and aspirations for myself were evaporating before my eyes. I was informed I could come back at any time, but I knew that dream had dried up into dust to be swirled away forever.

I was too naïve to understand all I was doing was putting a Band-aid on a bullet hole. Chuck and I continued to grow further and further apart, and after seven years my second marriage fell to pieces.

In life the partner who is by our side should be empowering you to achieve the highest apex you can climb to. When the person who professes to love you tries to dim or even snuff out your light, this is not the person who has your best interests at heart. If you don't love yourself enough to realize that, you'll continue to stay mired in lost opportunities and longing for what could have been. We should never strive to live for what could have been but for what can be, until it turns into what is and gives way to what's next. I learned this lesson far too late in life, sacrificing my what can be for what

I believed at the time was the greater good. While I can't go back and undo that decision, the best and most abundant gift I can give myself now is to never again put myself on hold for what I want out of life. I must stand strong with the courage of my convictions and keep walking toward the light of my dreams.

To my loving daughter, Kaytlin Breanne Bonner, from your adoring mother, Jennie—with all my love.

Kaytlin,

I want you to know how dear to me you are and may you always have this letter close to your heart. I have thought and thought of how to tell you how much you mean to me, and decided the best way for me to express my thoughts to you would be in a letter. This letter serves many purposes: One is to tell you how special you are, so that anytime you may feel otherwise you may reread it as a reminder. Second is to reinforce why I do the things I do as a mother. And finally is to express my love to you unconditionally.

Kaytlin, you are a gift from God. You are my only daughter and I awaited your arrival with so much anticipation. I was so excited to know I was going to get a princess to love and share all the things mothers and daughters get to experience. We are able to share makeup tips, clothing style, hairdos, and all the ups and downs of dating experiences. You are a dynamic personality and so full of life. Kaytlin, you are a force of energy that no one forgets, and you have a charisma that emanates long after you've gone. It must be amazing to know people think of how funny and amazing you are even after you have left their presence.

I can't wait to go through this life with you and see what an amazing young woman you grow into. Yes, Kaytlin, you are beautiful, creative, very intelligent, and strong willed. I see you as an asset to any company or organization. Kaytlin, you can achieve and do anything you want to do. Kaytlin, you have the capability to become and be anything you dream in this life. I am so proud to be your mother and await your success with anticipation. Kaytlin, you have shown me your compassion and mothering tendencies. You are a person of great heartfelt thought and empathy toward others. You love with all you have within you, and give 100 percent to the people you love. Kaytlin, you are strong and stand up for what you believe in, and I am glad to know that you don't allow anyone to step over what you believe without speaking your mind. These qualities are just the tip of the iceberg of who you are, Kaytlin, and the endless possibilities of what you are capable of accomplishing. YOU ARE AMAZING in every area of your life and I am glad you are my daughter.

I know there are times when you think I am being a pain. However, everything I do for you is out of love. Boundaries are things we must all learn and have in place to succeed in this world; without them the world would be a wreck. I only want what's best for you, and with these boundaries I hope you choose to learn that any effort you give for your life is given back to you tenfold. Sometimes the effort deals with action and sometimes it's simply remaining silent and being still for guidance.

I know that one of these days, you will look back and say, "Thank you, Mom, for seeing so much more in me than what I could see at the time. Thank you for caring for me so much that setting boundaries was an effort to protect me from hidden dangers I lacked knowledge of at the time. Thank you for providing insight on how to be disciplined in order to achieve. I really appreciate and love you, Mom, for everything good you gave me and what I thought at the time was BAD."

You see, Kaytlin, I was you at one time and felt that sometimes my parents were being unfair. However, as I grew into a young woman the things they taught me helped me become the productive, successful, and happy person I am today.

Now, if there ever comes a day you want to stay with someone else or someone else comes into your life, I hope that you will come to me with clear, sound reasons that we can discuss. I love you and I would never hold you hostage or keep you for my personal benefit or gain. Always know that I choose not to keep you from your happiness. I chose my job as your mother to unconditionally groom you for a productive life full of happiness.

It is in my belief that whoever is in the best situation to fulfill and groom you into a beautiful woman is where you should be. Being a mother is being able to share your joys in life and your consequences, the ups and downs with you—that is what a mother does. It is what I do as your mother, and will continue to do for the rest of my life.

You are now reaching the age of becoming a young woman. Whether it hurts or not, we must always tell each other the truth so that we can continue our journey as mother and daughter. The gift God gave me was you, Kaytlin, and in return I give you the gift of a life filled with unconditional love and the ability to become anything you wish to be without restraint.

I love you always,
Mom

CHAPTER 4

Enter Tommy

It is incumbent upon all of us to listen to the whispers—that gut feeling, that intuition that tells us when something is wrong, and when we should walk away. Had I listened more intently to my own whispers, I could have avoided paying a hefty emotional price.

The end of my seven-year marriage with Chuck was one of the most devastating events I would ever go through in life. However, none of us should ever stay in situations where we don't enjoy one hundred percent of our partners' support, and given that, we oftentimes must make hard choices for our ultimate health and happiness.

It is ironic that after convincing me to abandon my budding legal career, Chuck would represent my first experience with ongoing custody issues. He made the decision to bring suit against me for custody of our daughter, although he admitted to me later that he'd only done it because he felt like he had to, not because he really wanted to. He lost his bid for custody, and eventually we were able to work out a regular agreement to allow him to spend time with Kaytlin.

Our eventual custody arrangement would serve as a ripple effect, the reverberations of which I would experience for years to come. Our agreement mandated I stay in the Montgomery County area (a suburb of Houston), where we had resided for the better part of our marriage. My first choice would have been to return home to the Dallas area so I could be closer to my family. I drew strength from those connections, and as I embarked upon yet another evolution in my life I wanted to surround myself with those bonds. I couldn't have known the path that lay waiting for me as a result of being bound to an area I did not consider to be my home; I couldn't have known I would fall prey to the machinations of a manipulative charmer, resetting yet again the course of my journey.

As is my way, I concentrated on making the best of a bad situation and looked at it as an opportunity. I forged ahead with a new career in pharmaceutical sales, a career that would allow me to develop solutions for doctors and their patients, and one that melded quite well with my outgoing and competitive nature. In fact it was this new career path that led me to Tommy.

I met Tommy through his mother, Patsy, during a routine sales call with one of my regular doctors; she was a patient in the waiting room and quite persistent that I was exactly the type of girl her son would date. She struck up a conversation with me, fawning all over me about how beautiful I was and how I would be perfect for her son, who she claimed was quite handsome. No matter how much I resisted, she persisted—she wasn't about to let me walk out of there without some exchange of information. While I would not take her son's phone number, I relented and gave her mine. She was quite excited, promising he would call me soon. I held no expectations for any future romance with her son; in truth I was still healing from the trauma of my divorce. I was not looking for any romantic entanglements during that time in my life.

I was surprised to hear from Tommy a few days later, and we hit it off right away. Over the next two weeks, we talked three to four hours a day; he was charming and funny, and our conversations flowed with the ease of two people who'd known each other forever. It wasn't long before we decided to meet in person, and, as Patsy had said, Tommy was quite good looking—jet-black hair, piercing hazel eyes like his mother, and a lean, chiseled body. He brought me flowers on our first date and oozed sophistication and charisma from every pore.

I fell for Tommy quite fast, egged on by his lavish attention and dedication to wining and dining me, taking me to only the finest restaurants. I was giddy from the devotion he displayed, and admittedly it felt wonderful to have someone show me that kind of attention and affection. I found him to be an honest and open man, which besides his obvious physical attributes held a strong fascination for me. He also forged a gentle bond with Kaytlin, playing upon her love of horses by taking us riding several times during the eight months we were together. I'm ashamed to admit he bamboozled us with his charms.

Another strong component of my relationship with Tommy was the bond I built with his family. I was so far away from my own family, seeing how close he was to his own warmed my heart, and even more so when I was included in their outings.

I was so overwhelmed by Tommy's generosity and the warmth of his family that I ignored the whispers, that little voice telling me something was not right. Even as the voice grew to a deafening howl, I still would not heed the warnings and follow my instincts to leave the relationship behind. He informed me he was a pot smoker and he would never give up the habit that had formed during his adolescence. My stance was not to judge him, but rather to mandate he keep it away from me and my children. Had I been listening to the whispers, I would have come to the logical conclusion that this was not an individual I should have been associating with. Oftentimes people will provide windows into their true selves by revealing even the most inconsequential details.

I believe at our cores we want to think the best about people, and we never want to be thought of as judgmental or condescending. It is holding fast to this attitude that causes us to brush aside warning signs both big and small, and in the end causes irreparable damage to our lives. Our ultimate responsibility is to ourselves and what allows us to lay our heads in peace against our pillows each night, not that we refuse to judge people for their actions, believing their transgressions to be insignificant or somehow not affecting us. Every action has a reaction, even those we do not do ourselves. The actions of those around us can have far-reaching impacts.

Tommy's true colors began to shine through with brilliant clarity, though I just refused to take off the blinders. He became fixated with the idea of our conceiving a child together; I made it clear to him that I would not entertain the notion of having a child outside of marriage. He would not be dissuaded so easily, and in the course of pursing his scheme he would continue to reveal his dark side to me in dramatic bits and pieces. He attempted to pressure me into performing sexual acts that made me uncomfortable, including bringing in another woman—or man—into bed with us. He insisted we would have to indulge in these experiences together before he would ever consider proposing marriage to me. I finally began to listen to the whispers and realized it was not in my best interest to continue seeing this man, so I cut all ties with him.

Tommy became quite insistent with me about our future, dangling the carrot of marriage in front of me, leading me to believe, quite wrongly, that no man would ever provide for me the way he could. I turned the whispers down and allowed him to woo me back to his side. I held firm to the belief that we could work on our issues and build a solid, long-lasting bond with each other. I still wanted a stable family, and I was naïve enough to think this man would be the one to supply it.

I was in quicksand by then, sinking ever deeper into the depths of Tommy's deceit. He tricked me into going to a strip club with him, even going so far as to hire a dancer to provide us both with a private dance, which I refused. Tommy, however, took no such pass, and violated this woman right in front of me. I was disgusted with him, and disgusted with myself for allowing myself to be degraded like that. The next day I washed my hands of the whole situation, finally able to stand strong and walk away from Tommy's depravity.

It wasn't long after that incident that I began to feel queasy, and I suspected Tommy's fervent wish to have a child with me might have been coming true. Indeed the doctor confirmed my suspicion, sending me into a state of panic. Having a child out of wedlock breached every one of my beliefs; I am a strong proponent of marriage, and it would never be my first choice to bring an innocent life into this world without the benefit of a loving and happy home with two caring and committed parents. I also had my daughter to think about—this wasn't the example I wanted to set for her as a young lady. Of course I worried about how my family would react, as I was not raised to be a woman who would have a child outside of marriage.

After much prayer and reflection, I realized I was strong enough emotionally and spiritually to mother this child. I had the money; I had a good job and a beautiful home. I would bring this baby into the world. Chuck and I hadn't used birth control throughout our marriage, and aside from Kaytlin I'd never conceived, which convinced me I wasn't meant to have any more children. I considered this baby to be a blessing, and once I made that shift in my thinking it was with great anticipation that I proceeded with my pregnancy and awaited the birth of my child.

Tommy's reaction to my news was to propose marriage, which I declined. While I knew Tommy was not meant to be my husband, I felt quite strongly that he should be involved in every aspect of the child's life. I had visions of being friends and successful co-parents, hosting birthday parties together, and celebrating our child's milestones.

Initially, Tommy went to doctor's appointments with me, and Patsy even came along. She was super excited about the baby and wanted to be involved in every aspect. About two and a half months into the pregnancy, Tommy dropped off the face of the earth. I tried to keep him and his family involved with my progress, sending them sonograms and giving them updates on my doctor's appointments. I invited Patsy and his sister, Stephanie, to my baby shower. It ripped my heart out when they called me the day before to tell me they had attended a funeral that day and were too drained to celebrate my baby coming into this world. I couldn't understand how they could be so cruel, and hoped it wouldn't spill over to this new life I was nurturing.

Although the relationship with Tommy did not work

out, I had always thought Patsy and I had a special bond with each other. She always included me in shopping trips and outings with the family, and considering those memories we shared it was hurtful when she began to show signs of disdain toward me. She would drop accusations, questioning the paternity of my unborn child and slamming my decisions regarding Kylan's care and upbringing. Kylan was being raised by my parents, and at the time it was the right thing to do for all of us.

Patsy tried to make the situation shameful when the truth was I never tried to hide Kylan or the situation with him from anyone. He still called me Mom, and I talked to him all the time. It infuriated me that she tried to twist the situation around to make me look like a bad mother.

My son, Kylan

People who haven't been around me much are sometimes surprised to hear I have four children, not three.

After I left Dana and moved home with my family, Dana and I shared custody of our son, and it was during one of Kylan's visitation weekends with his father that my little boy's life changed forever.

Dana's new girlfriend called early one morning,

insisting I come and get Kylan. As I raced to get my son, my mind was filled with all sorts of terrible thoughts as to what could have happened. When I arrived and looked into my son's eyes, it was clear something was terribly wrong with him. I was informed that he'd almost drowned that day during a fishing trip with Dana and his friends. Kylan had fallen out of the boat and into the water. Instead of jumping into the water to save him, Dana had been prepared to let him sink to the bottom. Fortunately Dana's friend had jumped in and pulled my son to safety.

I was horrified that Dana would allow his son to almost die, and I called my attorney the next morning to update him on this tragic turn of events. Dana displayed no remorse when questioned by the judge about his actions, and as a result the judge stripped my ex-husband of all his paternal rights. It would be sixteen years before he saw Kylan again.

As a consequence of being underwater so long, Kylan developed a life-threatening respiratory infection. In addition those few seconds he had spent underwater severely affected his motor skills, and he had seizures up until the time he was fifteen.

I was in school full-time and working two part-time jobs, so I was unable to afford proper health care to cover Kylan's mounting medical expenses. My parents stepped in and told me the best solution would be for them to adopt Kylan, which would give him access to their health care. After a lot of sleepless nights and prayer, I made the extremely difficult decision to turn legal custody of my son over to my parents.

As I said, this was not a choice I made lightly. I agonized hourly over whether or not this was the best thing to do. In the end, as much as I wanted him with me, his health was so precarious I knew it would be selfish of me to keep him from getting the best possible care, and at that time my parents were the best choice.

While Kylan lived with my parents, he always knew me as his mom. I visited him every other weekend; every holiday and every summer we were together. My parents and I never, ever hid the truth from him. As he got older and we would talk about things, he would tell me, "I've got my meemaw"— what he called my mother—"and my mom." He said he felt so lucky to have two of us. While we have not always been physically living together, he has always been my son.

Kylan is eighteen now, and because of the problems with his motor skills things have always been a little tougher for him. He gets winded easily, so he can't play most sports. In spite of that, he stands six foot three, weighs two hundred pounds, and has become a fantastic golfer. Even though he's had to work much harder than other kids his age, he's grown into the sweetest, caring, most thoughtful young man. Even better, he and Dana have begun to forge a good relationship. Dana reached out to me a few years ago and apologized for everything he'd done to Kylan and me. I know it bothered Kylan as he was growing up that he didn't have a relationship with his dad, but now they've really begun to change that fact. Dana takes Kylan to play golf, and they go out to dinner together, and have really been doing a lot more father-son activities.

Looking back, I do regret that I allowed my parents to adopt Kylan. I know now that I could have given them power of attorney and retained custody. But I was young and didn't know any better, and my parents dictated that this was the way it had to be. However, it was like I had the best of both worlds; Kylan got the critical medical care he needed, and I got to see him all the time. In fact, he's recently decided to come and live with me, and I couldn't be happier.

My relationship with Patsy continued to deteriorate as the insinuations about the baby's paternity and my mothering skills became more frequent and more vicious. I received a steady stream of hurtful e-mails from both Patsy and Stephanie, and worse was left to deal with all of it alone, as Tommy had disappeared. Shortly before the baby's birth,

Tommy reappeared with a new fiancée in tow, which added another layer of strain to an already difficult situation.

The stress of dealing with this tornado around me put me in preterm labor. My precious Aidan arrived the night before New Year's Eve, six weeks ahead of schedule, and had to go straight into the NICU. The tension only intensified as I had to deal with Tommy and his family's constant hovering around me and the baby. I was devastated when Patsy brought an unwrapped baby gift for Aidan while I was still in the hospital, and the box had monsters on each side with the words "MEAN GREEN SCUM REMOVER."

And yet they were saying the baby couldn't be Tommy's. One look at Aidan and there was no denying who he belonged to. Still, I subjected Aidan to the DNA test Tommy and his family insisted I have done, and, as I'd been saying all along, to nobody's surprise (except maybe Tommy's family's) Aidan was definitely Tommy's son.

Once I got the baby home and we'd established paternity, I worked quite hard to include Tommy and his family in Aidan's life, allowing them to spend two to three nights a week at my home with the baby. I never once tried to shut them out, and tried to be a gracious and welcoming hostess even as I was in the throes of breastfeeding and running on precious little sleep. Even with my bending over backward to accommodate them, I had to deal with e-mails like this one from Patsy:

*JENNIE, I WANT TO THANK YOU FOR SEND-
ING ME THE PICTURE OF AIDAN. HE IS A
BEAUTIFUL BABY BOY. IS THIS THE NAME
THAT IS ON HIS BIRTH CERTIFICATE? I
WOULD LOVE TO COME SEE HIM ANYTIME.
PLEASE CALL ME OR E-MAIL ME.*

LOVE, PATSY

*An old prospector walks his tired, old mule into
a Western town one day. The man had been out in
the desert for about six months without a drop of
whiskey. He walked up to the first saloon he came
to and tied his old mule to the hitch rail.*

*As he stood there brushing some of the dust
from his face and clothes, a gunslinger walked out
of the saloon with a gun in one hand and a bottle
of whiskey in the other. The gunslinger looked at
him and laughed, saying, "Hey, old man, have you
ever danced?"*

*The old man looked up at the gunslinger and
said, "No, I never did dance. I just never wanted
to."*

*A crowd had gathered by then, and the gun-
slinger said, "Well, you old fool, you're gonna dance
now," and started shooting at the old man's feet.*

*The old prospector was hopping around, and
everybody was laughing.*

*When the gunslinger fired his last bullet, he
holstered his gun and turned around to go back*

into the saloon. The old man reached up on the mule, drew his shotgun, and pulled both hammers back, making a double clicking sound.

The gunslinger heard the sound, and everything got quiet. The crowd watched as he slowly turned around, looking down both barrels of the shotgun.

The old man asked, "Did you ever kiss a mule square on the ass?"

The gunslinger swallowed hard and said, "No, but I've always wanted to."

MESSAGE: don't mess with us old farts.

Eventually, we settled into a comfortable enough though not ideal situation. I continued to be so naïve as to think Tommy and I could be good co-parents. I believed we would all work together to surround my beautiful little boy with nothing but love.

The first time Tommy dragged me into court was when Aidan was six months old. Tommy wanted to modify the existing court order to get more time with Aidan. I had primary custody, and Tommy had visitation. I was stunned because I was already giving him and his family more time than they were supposed to have. I let Tommy take Aidan on the first, third, and fifth weekends of the month, which was a lot of time for a newborn baby to be away from his mother. As was my way, I really tried to be lenient and the best person I could be in a situation that was far from perfect. I wanted Tommy and his family to continue to be a part of Aidan's life.

When we begin to make concessions in life to accommodate the wishes and desires of others, we give away too much of ourselves in the process. When we believe others hold the key to our happiness and security, we lose ourselves. The truth is while there are a lot of good people in the world who walk and talk with purity of spirit, there are just as many people who live with darkness in their hearts and use that evil intent to destroy the lives of those around them. I could live with hate in my heart toward Tommy and his family for everything they've done to me, but it would serve no purpose. Instead I must take the lessons they have taught me and use them for my greater good. While I will continue to believe the good, I will scratch the surface to see what lies beneath and look much more critically at those around me for hidden agendas and falsity of spirit. No one will look out for you but you.

CHAPTER 5

The Love of My Life

In the midst of my court battle with Tommy, I met the man who would be my greatest love and my greatest downfall.

I always compared the love Nick Morton and I shared to that of the characters in *The Notebook* because I could completely relate to the dynamics of that story. Nick and I had a lot of volatility, but there was love underneath it all.

> *They didn't agree on much. In fact, they didn't agree on anything. They fought all the time and challenged each other every day. But despite their differences, they had one important thing in common. They were crazy about each other.*
>
> —Nicholas Sparks

From the moment Nick and I met, we had undeniable chemistry. However, as time went on, I understood control was at the root of our relationship, namely the power he held over me. During our time together, we married and had a beautiful baby boy. Nick also threatened to make my life a living hell if I ever left him. Before it was all over, he pulled me, my friends, my family, and my children into a black hole of family court litigation.

Nick, being my love, of course knew all my secrets—all the things that would hurt me the most—and he did not hesitate to use each and every one of them against me. The people closest to us are the ones who have the power to hurt us the most. When you put your trust in the one you love, it's not a weakness; it's natural. If ever they should twist your vulnerabilities around to destroy you, it's not love. My parents always told me sticks and stones can break your bones, but words will never harm you. Well, that's only a little true. Hurtful words spoken to you by someone you love can cut to the bone. They can't take them back, and that cut doesn't always heal right.

At the time I met Nick, I was still living in Conroe, Texas, and embroiled in another nasty court case with Tommy regarding custody of Aidan. Nick moved into the house next door and a thunderbolt struck me. He was the most beautiful man I'd ever see in my life: sparkling blue eyes, hair the color of coal, and a body like granite. He was the man I saw in my dreams when I conjured up what my future husband would look like. I always told myself that when I saw the man I was meant to spend my life with, I would know it.

I knew that day I would marry Nick.

Nick began to pursue me, playing the part of the gentlemanly neighbor, doing everything from taking my trashcan to the curb to inviting me over for a drink. The attraction and chemistry that crackled in the air between us were as powerful as magnets, and, as much as I wanted to give into my physical desires, I held strong to my belief that it would not be a good idea to get involved with a neighbor. I was leery of the consequences if we gave in to those romantic feelings and the relationship didn't work out. I made the decision to maintain a proper distance from him.

Nick would not be discouraged, and stepped up his efforts to win me over. He showered me with compliments, flirted with me every chance he got, and made it clear he would propel me over to his side. The prophecy came to fruition, and I'm embarrassed to admit I engaged in a sexual relationship with him far too soon. I expected our first one-night liaison would be our last, but Nick continued to work his trickery on me, convincing me he wanted a relationship with me and I was special. What I experienced with Nick was unlike anything I'd ever felt before. There was an intensity and a passion between us I'd never known existed. What I came to realize much later was that, much the way Tommy had, Nick helped to fill a void in my life. Being with him gave me that family feeling, and he wanted to spend time with me and my kids.

I was done. For me Nick was it. He was the love of my life.

*I finally understood what true love meant…love
meant that you care for another person's happiness
more than your own, no matter how painful the
choices you face might be.*

—Nicholas Sparks

Much like it had been with Tommy, I once again ignored
the whispers and the red flags, strapping blinders to my face
and ignoring all the obvious warning signs that Nick was not
who he claimed to be. The litany of deceptions visited upon
me by Nick is stunning to me now as I look back on it. I only
saw what I wanted to see, and I allowed the intense physi-
cality of our relationship to overrule all rational thought, and
relied instead on the perception he wanted me to have of
him. He was a manipulator who lied as easily as he breathed,
from everything about his age (he said he was twenty-six
when in reality he was twenty-four) to the real nature of our
relationship.

When you're dating someone, it's a natural expectation
that you will go out in public and participate in the normal
dating rituals of dinners and movies. Where Tommy had
wined and dined me, Nick spent many nights at my home.
I rationalized it to myself by declaring he was a homebody
just like myself. This played in to my ever-present longing for
stability and normalcy. Nick knew my weaknesses, and he
used them to his advantage. Even his friends could see what
I refused to admit—that he was using me and keeping me
hidden away from the rest of the world, never even acknowl-
edging me as his girlfriend. Yet I continued to be won over

by his persistent declarations of love and devotion, wanting so much to believe in him and the words he spoke.

I refused to see the real Nick or the situation we were in with regard to our relationship. It had been my dream to marry Nick, and he made it plain that he couldn't see himself settling down, especially with someone who already had children. It was extremely important to him that he go through the experience of having a baby with a woman who didn't already have children, and he said his family would be mortified if he were ever with a woman in my position.

The pain of his words and attitude was too much to bear, and I made the painful decision to leave the relationship. Nick was not ready to let me go, and became quite persistent in his efforts to rekindle the flame between us. He even went so far as to tell me Tommy had reached out to him, but vowed he would protect me from him. It would be to my detriment that I didn't give this declaration much thought. Not heeding those words was a mistake I would regret dearly. I stood strong and refused to buckle under to a man who was not ready to be with me 100 percent.

And then I got pregnant.

Nick's insistence that he wasn't ready to settle down, particularly with me, sent me into an emotional tailspin. I had already violated my own values by getting pregnant with Aidan without the benefit of marriage, though in no way do I regret the decision to have him. However, I could not believe I had allowed myself to be pulled into this situation once again.

Nick, of course, was not happy. He reminded me that

he wasn't ready to settle down and that his family would disown him. I knew he didn't want to marry me, and under those circumstances I didn't want to be the mother of three children with no husband. In the end we made the painful decision to end the pregnancy.

CHAPTER 6

For Worse
or For Worse

As fate would have it, there was another baby waiting for me, and no matter what Nick's reaction, I would keep it. I told him we were having a baby, and this time there would be no talking me out of it.

I really was thrilled to begin the process of welcoming another new life into my family. Part of my excitement stemmed from my belief that Nick would see the light and ask me to marry him. I hoped the pregnancy would bring us closer together and seal our bond. In fact it only seemed to drive us further apart, and Nick was very often nowhere to be found, disappearing for days on end even though we lived next door to each other. This began the off-and-on nature of our relationship, where one minute it would be like the old days and we were together all the time, then in the blink of an eye he would vanish, leaving me to wonder when I would see him again. Against my better judgment, I would welcome him back with open arms each and every time. I had convinced myself he was the love of my life and we belonged together. I craved every inch of this man's body and soul and would take whatever scraps he threw me.

No woman should ever be satisfied with being second best on a man's list no matter the circumstance. I believe all women think deep down they will be the one to convince a man to change his ways and settle down. We all feel we're "the one," and in that pursuit we will endure a multitude of humiliations and turn blind eyes to the disrespect men unworthy of our true selves show us. We have to love and respect ourselves if we can ever hope for anyone to reciprocate those same emotions. Not having a strong sense of self is a weakness and will leave you vulnerable to the manipulations of those who don't wish you well.

Our strongest desire in life should be to love ourselves first and foremost; it is only when we accomplish that we can hope to give and receive such a blessing with another person. Making the mistake of thinking another person will complete the circle of happiness for you, and pinning all your hopes and dreams onto the whim of another, is a recipe for self-destruction. I didn't love myself enough; otherwise I wouldn't have been so receptive to Nick's treachery toward me. Had I concentrated more effort on respecting and understanding who I was, I wouldn't have lost myself and so much more.

I thought my deepest dreams had finally come true when Nick asked me to marry him; I was elated because in my mind I had waited to receive the gift, and it was now coming to pass. Finally all of the doubt and suspicion would be replaced by the reality of a happy and loving home where we would raise our child together and provide a secure environment in which our family unit would thrive. My happiness knew no bounds.

However I was heartbroken when Nick told me he wanted to get married right away and whisked me off to the Montgomery County Courthouse, where we eloped. It was so important to me that Nick and I say our vows in front of his family and friends, as he had kept me hidden from them for most of our relationship. I did not want or need a huge ceremony—just Nick and me with God as our witness. I felt a proper ceremony would be Nick's declaration to the world—"I love this woman." It would be a commitment that made it clear to those around us that he knew his life could not be better without me by his side, and the more people who witnessed our vows to honor each other the better.

However, I would not get that promise from Nick. He refused to follow the traditions of a wedding, and to rub salt in the wound I was informed I couldn't tell anyone about our nuptials. What should have been the happiest time of my life was being carried out under the cover of darkness and shame. I had foolishly believed marriage would change Nick. For all intents and purposes, I was pregnant and alone.

The indignities would continue as I learned about

ongoing infidelities, endured disappearing acts, and experienced physical venom I hadn't seen since the dark years of my marriage to Dana. There were times when Nick choked me down to the ground, threatened me with the pistol he kept in his truck, promised to kill me and anyone close to me, ripped my hair out, and hit me in the head with a flashlight, causing me to develop a crippling migraine. I called 911 multiple times for help, but it seemed nothing could stop his rampages against me. He had turned into a monster, and all I could do was pray for the storm to pass.

Even as Nick disrespected me with other women and physically abused me, I continued to want to hold him close and still hoped he would show me love and kindness. I wanted a full-time husband, not a man who used our home as a weigh station and came and left as the spirit moved him. I held fast to the belief that our love would prevail.

⸻

A Woman's Love

I tried to make Nick understand the value of a woman's love and how nothing in the world can ever compare. It is pure and unconditional. A woman will walk on water for her man. She will see the diamond in the rough and defend her man to the death even if she isn't convinced he is right. She will hang on her man's every word even when he isn't saying anything worth listening to. No matter how many times her friends tell her that man is no good, or how many times her man slams the door on the relationship, she will still be there waiting to give her very best and then some. She will continue to try to win her man's heart even when her man has done everything he can to convince her she isn't good enough. A woman's love will stand the test of time, logic, and all circumstances.

A real man will show his woman he loves her by practicing the three Ps: PROFESS, PROVIDE, and PROTECT. If these three simple actions are not present in a relationship, then it is not true, real, and lasting love.

When a man PROFESSES, he will shout from the rooftops, "This is my lady!" This is an official title that extends far beyond just being a friend. This shows the special place a man has reserved in his heart for his lady by bestowing the title upon her. It sends a message to other men that this particular lady is off limits.

Once a man declares his love for his woman, he PROVIDES by doing everything he can to support his lady and their family—emotionally, spiritually, physically and financially. This is a man's purpose in life. The only time a man will have his hand out to his lady is when he is showing her support, when he is showing her affection, and when he is showing her that she is his. He will always have her best interests at heart, and will ensure she has everything she needs by putting food on the table and keeping the lights on. This only boosts his prowess as a man—this is what makes him a real man. His own needs will be secondary; having a new boat or a night out on the town with his buddies will pale in comparison to providing for his loved ones. Material possessions cannot make a man puff out his chest with pride or square his shoulders with respect the way true appreciation and adoration from a woman can. Ask any real man not doing right by his family what his biggest regret is and they will say, "I wish I had the ability to provide better."

The natural, most basic instinct of a man for his woman is to PROTECT her. Perhaps above all others this is the most important thing to a woman, to know that her man will fight anyone to the death for disparaging her in any way. Any male on the planet who truly loves and respects his mate will obliterate anyone or anything that offends his woman. Indeed this is what every man should be willing to do for the woman he professes to love and provides for. All women want this from their men because that is what girls have been raised to expect—they count on the most important men in their lives to protect them and keep them safe from harm no matter the cost.

I suffered through all of this while still pregnant with our child, and the stress of Nick's actions sent my blood pressure through the roof, necessitating my doctor's ordering me on bed rest. During my bed rest, Hurricane Ike—a category 4 hurricane that caused 112 deaths in the United States—tore through Montgomery County. Instead of staying home with me and my two children—including a toddler—Nick disappeared for three days during the storm, not returning my phone calls and text messages. On the third night, he finally resurfaced, reeking of liquor and carelessness. I was in hysterics by then, demanding to know where he'd been and why he'd left me in such a precarious situation. I almost went into pre-term labor I was so upset.

However, Nick couldn't have cared less. He showed a disturbing lack of affect over the severity of the situation. Instead of remorse my outrage over his behavior triggered a venomous attack on my pregnancy and how being with me had ruined his life. He screamed at me, "I am shutting the baby-making money factory down!" He declared he had nothing to live for and took his gun, threatening to shoot himself. In a panic I called his parents, begging them to find and save Nick. Fortunately they located him. It wasn't long after this episode that they began to display considerable coldness toward me. It was all too much to bear, and I made the decision to file for divorce.

Once Nick found out I was planning to leave him, his true character began to reveal itself to me in frightening bits and pieces. You never want to believe the one you love the most will be the one to hurt you the most. You never think the man you share your hopes and dreams with, the man you pledged to spend your life with, will turn into a monster. I was miles away from family, alone and defenseless against a man who could and would break me in two. He told me if I ever left him, he would make my children and me pay dearly, promising to take them away from me. I knew this was not an empty threat; Nick came from a wealthy, highly connected political family who used their business to buy and trade for political influence and put officials in their pockets. Years earlier they had taken a child away from a brother-in-law, an outsider, so I knew they could do the same to me.

The family also used their money to control Nick, dictating the manner in which they would dole it out to help him start his insurance business or pressuring him to marry the type of woman they found acceptable. They were an extremely tight-knit clan, all living within minutes of each other and never having lived outside of Montgomery County. No one dared go against them, least of all anyone in the family, for they would suffer the consequences of doing so.

Nick lived in fear of disappointing his family, knowing if he didn't go along with their every whim he would be made to pay. He would face banishment from the family and have his source of income—which they supplied—cut off. He felt he had no choice but to comply with their wishes, even if it meant sacrificing me and our relationship. I've had girlfriends say to me they believed that were it not for the suffocating influence of his family, Nick would have stepped up to the plate and had the courage to be with me in the manner a man should be with a woman he loves.

While I agree with that to some extent, the truth is Nick was incapable of love. With the passage of time and much reflection and prayer, I can see that Nick has a narcissistic personality. Narcissists are inept when it comes to feeling true emotion, particularly with regard to romantic relationships. They don't know how to love because they don't know how to feel. They react to criticism with rage, shame, or humiliation; take advantage of other people to achieve their own goals; have excessive feelings of self-importance; exaggerate their achievements and talents; have unreasonable expectations of favorable treatment; need constant attention and admiration; disregard the feelings of others; have little ability to feel empathy; have obsessive self-interests; and pursue mainly selfish goals. It didn't matter what I did or did not do. Nick would never love me because he was incapable of feeling love.

By the same token, once he knew I was rejecting and divorcing him, he became obsessed with me. He turned on the charm and devotion, wooing me back all over again. Narcissists are quite clever in the way they suck you in. They're able to tap in to your vulnerabilities and use them against you while taking power from you and using it to further their own agendas. We're powerless against them and don't realize until it's too late the ways in which they've mentally abused us.

Unbelievably, with all this drama swirling around me, I

delivered another healthy, beautiful baby boy who I named Hunter. I was still operating under the fantasy that this would be enough to keep Nick at home and a part of our family. Nothing changed. Once again Nick was never home, and yet again I was home alone with the baby.

What I didn't know was that during this time he was plotting with Tommy to turn the tables against me. Nick convinced Tommy to become his coconspirator in order to team up against me to take me down. Together they would turn my life against me, all with the goal of eviscerating me until there was nothing left. It was part of Nick's master plan to trigger a series of events that would cause me to lose custody of Aidan and Hunter. As it turned out, for the better part of a year Nick had been calling Tommy on a regular basis and cooking up all kinds of schemes against me. Tommy's family was also highly connected and still harbored grudges against me from the time I was pregnant. They wanted my little boy, and would do anything they could to get him. It wasn't long before Nick and Tommy had me back in court for the biggest fight of my life.

CHAPTER 7

The Nightmare Continues

The humiliations I continued to suffer at Nick's hands had become unbearable. He kept me isolated from my friends and family, continued to pull disappearing acts, and made it quite clear he never intended to be a real husband to me.

I could no longer live under this cloud of terror; he was a very real and very present threat to the safety of me and all my children, including his own son. I could not and would not endanger the lives of my children. Unbelievably, in spite of everything, I couldn't find it within myself to end the marriage, but Nick had no such problem, as he had me served with divorce papers. As if to make his point that he would hurt me at any cost, he knocked me down in a rage and declared he was taking Hunter away from me. I ran to grab my son, who was only a few weeks old, and Nick's response was to pull the baby by his feet, wrenching him from my arms. In the ruckus my nanny was able to take Hunter away from Nick, though unfortunately Aidan witnessed the entire ordeal.

By that point I'd been back at work for two days after taking maternity leave, and was in the throes of post-pregnancy hormonal fluctuations, not to mention I had just weaned Hunter from breastfeeding, so we were both in a completely vulnerable state. I felt my world collapsing around me as I watched Nick continue his attempts to take Hunter. Worse still, Nick's father came barreling through the door to aid his son in this cruel act. Desperate, I called 911 for help. Fortunately, they came out and were able to prevent Nick and his father from absconding with my son. It wasn't until much later, when I was coming home after running some errands, that I remembered seeing Nick's brother that day hanging around the entrance to my community. A chill passed through my spine as I realized the entire scene had been preplanned.

Although the acts of filing for divorce and moving out for good would make it seem as though Nick wanted nothing to do with me, he still wanted the utmost control over my life and my every move. Nick began to stalk me, driving outside my home countless times a day, following me, and hiring private detectives to track me from morning to night. He broke into my home on numerous occasions. He would bang on my door and scream obscenities at me at all hours of the night, calling me a bad mother. He began to frequent my friend's places of business in an attempt to terrify them. I got phone calls on a daily basis from friends and acquaintances informing me of the wretched things Nick was saying about me, and about his stealthy activities. This was on top of the masterful way he'd infiltrated Tommy's family, passing on his malice toward me through them. I became a psychic during this time, as I could predict with near accuracy who would call me when and what they would say. The telephone chain would typically start with Nick, followed by a call from Tommy, then his mother, Patsy, and finally a call from his wife, Karen. It was an ongoing, methodical, emotional assault that left me emotionally drained.

This continued harassment frightened my children to the point they were afraid to go out in the front yard to play. I couldn't even take them to the park because every time I attempted to do so Nick would show up, and I would have to turn around and head home for fear of what he might say or do in front of the kids.

He sent me harassing text messages, and anytime I had visitors at my home, either male or female, he would have them followed and run background and credit checks on them. During one instance he choked me down to the ground and took off with my cell phone. Once in possession of my cell phone, he called every male name he found—including the names of sales contacts and doctors I worked with—and threatened to kick their asses or visit other bodily harm upon them. These actions terrified my children, and I began the process of trying to get protective orders.

I had numerous witnesses to the acts Nick perpetrated

against me, and voice recordings via the countless calls I made to 911. I worked diligently to gather evidence of Nick's violent tendencies toward me, and filed harassment and stalking charges with the Montgomery County Police. I felt blessed when one of the officers who came to my house remembered my first 911 call. She recalled how crazy Nick had been acting—so much so she'd pulled her gun on him. As he'd played what he was sure would be his trump card: the "don't you know who I am and who my family are?" refrain. She told me she didn't care. She'd dealt with this type of behavior in her own family, and because she was familiar with it she would pursue Nick with everything she had.

She advised me to gather all my evidence and bring it to her the following day, and she would submit it. Relieved I'd finally found someone to hear my pleas, I rushed to the police department only to be told the officer had been removed from the case, and another officer had been assigned. I was further dismayed when the new officer showed blatant disregard for me and my evidence. After this ordeal I began the search for a high-powered attorney in Montgomery County to take my case. Doors were slammed in my face, and attorneys would not speak to me because they'd already been in contact with the Mortons. In essence I was blackballed.

Nick and his father paid me another visit at home, bringing with them more threats and the determination to shatter me into a million little pieces. To my eternal regret, my daughter, Kaytlin, jumped into the fray that day. After I called 911, Nick vowed he would lie to the police that I had assaulted him. Poor Kaytlin, so upset over Nick's behavior, screamed at him to stop lying and pleaded with him to stop hitting and hurting me. Nick's father launched a verbal tirade against me, and he and his son both spit on me. I was appalled by their vile words and actions. I never would have imagined they would stoop to such lows.

True to his word, Nick revealed a scratch mark on his arm, claiming it was from me. My pleas to the officer that there was no way I could have done that fell on deaf ears. The officer seemed reluctant to issue me a ticket; nevertheless, I was slapped with an assault charge.

My attorney dropped a bomb on me the next day: Nick and his attorney, Grady James, had gone to court to get a protective order against me. I was stunned. After all the times I had begged for protective orders against him, he'd now twisted the situation to his advantage. Yet again Nick had laid out a well-orchestrated campaign to turn the tables on me, and thus my attorney warned me to stay away from Nick.

"They are trying to set you up," my attorney said.

Once the 911 recordings were released and Nick's diabolical plot was revealed, he had no choice but to drop the assault charges against me. Of course he would continue to bully me, and my successive 911 calls to report these incidents were immediately followed by calls Nick made to police to give his side of the story, effectively turning everything into a "he said, she said" situation. I worked diligently to gather evidence of Nick's violent tendencies toward me, and retained yet another attorney to help me get a protective order. When the judge handed down an ex parte protective order, I thought my prayers had been answered and my luck was finally changing. My euphoria was short lived, as Nick violated the order that day in front of my mom, a friend, and Kaytlin. Once again I had to call 911 for help. The police were dismissive, calling my protective order nothing more than an expensive piece of paper that would be filed under G for garbage. We were all devastated, and by that point all we could do was cry.

During the protective order trial, the second attorney I hired, Kent Shriver, produced a false final divorce decree stating I could not move out of my home until Hunter was eighteen years old. This fraudulent document originated through Nick's attorney, Grady James. Mr. James is quite well known in Montgomery County and has earned a reputation as a cutthroat attorney who will stop at nothing to win a case. Retaining him to represent you means megabucks have been shelled out.

Mr. Shriver used the document to coerce me into dropping the stalking charges and prevent me from pursing a protective order against Nick. I was amazed he would attempt this, as he had heard the plethora of audio tapes of Nick threatening to kill me and anyone around me. Anytime I would question him about his legal strategy, or whether or not he planned to interview key witnesses for my case—such as my nanny, Kenzie—about the things they saw Nick and his family do to me and Kaytlin, Mr. Shriver would hit the roof and yell at me that he knew what he was doing. Once he began to pace nervously between the waiting room and the courtroom where we were sitting. Each time he came back to see me, he would try to convince me to drop the charges. As he continued his coercive tactics, my witnesses grew anxious, and I was plagued by an uneasy feeling. This was not good. Something was not right. Finally he pulled me aside and said Kenzie claimed she didn't want to testify. This was patently untrue, as she'd told me on several occasions she was more than willing to testify on my behalf, and further she'd never even spoken to Mr. Shriver as he claimed. All day I stood unwavering in my determination to go to trial. Eventually we were told to come back the next day, when the trial would resume.

We arrived the next morning fresh and ready to begin, only to be met with more insistence from my attorney that it was better for me to forgo a trial. My girlfriend could see this constant needling was wearing on me, and she got angry over his lack of regard for the situation, finally chiming in that we were going to trial.

Mr. Shriver pulled me in front of the Mortons and said, "Jennie, I like you, but you'd better tell your friend to shut up." I couldn't believe his behavior. The final blow was struck when he produced the falsified decree. This unscrupulous attorney had strung me along, leading me to believe he was acting as an advocate on my behalf, when in reality the case was a done deal before I even entered the courtroom.

I later uncovered evidence that Mr. Shriver was feeding

information about my case to Ms. Esposito and Mr. James,
violating attorney-client privilege. There were several occasions where he would ask me for more money, claiming he
was going to visit Mr. James's office. There were times when
his words to me were so harsh, even his paralegal would
gasp in disbelief over the way he was speaking to me and his
overall demeanor toward me. I felt trapped; I had paid him
almost $40,000 within a two-month period. Coupled with
the stress of the stalking/harassing behavior, fighting battles
in two separate courts simultaneously, and taking care of
three kids and a full-time career, I just didn't know what to
do.

When it came time to head to court more than a year
later, Nick was on a first-name basis with everyone at the
Montgomery County Courthouse, including the court staff.
He was cocky, almost as if he knew things I didn't. There were
numerous occasions where, after my protective order was
dropped and I would go to court to try to reinstate it, I would
notice court personnel speaking to Nick about our case.
There were even instances where attorneys would approach
me to ask if the Morton family was "still giving [me] hell."
I was devastated to see Nick had subpoenaed many of my
neighbors, Kaytlin's private counselors, and her dad. During
my testimony my parents sat outside the courtroom; later
they told me of the stream of judges that had come over to
shake the hand of Nick's father.

I was ripped to shreds on the witness stand. I was called a

liar for mentioning a DWI that Nick had on his record (and was later expunged), and told that I couldn't speak of anything prior to the last court order concerning Nick, although incidents in my past were dredged up and twisted around in horrifying detail. When it came time to present my documented evidence, it was conveniently "forgotten," or was not allowed to be submitted, which meant my case fell apart. Nick and his witnesses perjured themselves on the stand time and time again, and his attorneys knowingly submitted altered evidence on his behalf while other key witnesses were sent home from the trial, never to be questioned. It wasn't until later in the day that I realized this had happened, leaving my custody case in utter shambles. My attorney did not act in the best interest of my children, and bled me dry. I was left to fend for myself against these vultures.

I tried everything I could think of to turn the tide. I reached out to the district attorney's office, the Texas Rangers (a major division within the Texas Department of Public Safety that is charged with the investigation of major crime incidents and public corruption investigations), even the FBI only to be turned away once they found out who I was. Nick and his family had dismantled my good name with stunning swiftness and precision while manipulating even the highest authorities to turn a blind eye to the casualty of war, the person they'd been sworn to protect. It was all about money and influence, and I didn't have either.

In the midst of all of this, I was battling Tommy for

custody of Aidan—all because Nick had been working with him to make good on his threat: "I am going to break you and take your kids away." Tommy hadn't been around much, though things had been copacetic between us with regard to Aidan's custody. However, with Nick's prodding, Tommy sued me for custody despite our previous arrangement, through which I retained sole custody of Aidan, with Tommy having extended visitation. After the protective-order debacle, Nick's pursuit of Hunter intensified, further complicating my legal woes and my stress level.

Nick's stalking was not limited to me; he wreaked havoc on those around me. He threatened to shoot me in front of Kaytlin, and conspired with her dad, Chuck, as well as Tommy to bring me down. He even had his own father show up unauthorized at her school on several occasions, causing her severe psychological stress and necessitating the administration of medication to help ease her burden, along with continued counseling. Nick and Tommy would show up at daycare facilities where I had the little ones, causing a ruckus, and made harassing phone calls to the workers as well. Tommy would either bring Aidan back to me late—up to five hours past the appointed drop-off time—or not at all. The impetus for the continued coordinated outbursts at the daycare center was the opposing desires of both men where childcare was concerned; Tommy wanted Aidan in daycare while Nick wanted Hunter kept at home.

Trying to appease these two opposing forces was impossible, and made my life a living hell. My live-in nanny witnessed Nick's rages against me, his accusations that I had stolen a private journal from him, his constant harassing texts, and the multiple times he broke into the house. He also left her nasty, vile messages, and even went so far one time as to shove her out of the way when she tried to intervene during one of his rampages. He told her he would hurt her if she ever testified on my behalf, and went to her husband's place of business to threaten him, nearly costing this innocent bystander his job. Any person I was around, no matter how casually, was subjected to background checks, surveillance courtesy of private investigators hired by Nick, trumped-up warrants, losing their jobs, the destruction of their reputations, and even being railroaded out of town.

I learned later that much of Nick's stalking and harassment of me was partially mandated by his attorney, Ms. Esposito, and his previous attorney, Mr. James. After he dropped the assault charge, Nick pled with me to take him back, admitting Mr. James had instructed him to scratch himself so it would incriminate me and thus allow him to gain custody of Hunter. I was appalled by these unprovoked, vicious tactics; I am a good mother and was doing nothing wrong. I never kept my children from their fathers, and Aidan and Hunter were both well kept and taken care of. I know Nick and his attorneys were scrounging for dirt on me because they had nothing whatsoever to hang on me—no arrests, no drug use, no excessive drinking, not even a speeding ticket in sixteen years. Ms. Esposito also became the co-counsel in Tommy's case, and she instructed Nick on how to gather incriminating evidence against me using my own cell phone through an elaborate phone-tapping system.

As I began to spend more time in court, I realized the questions being asked by opposing counsel were rather pointed, and suggested that somehow they had been privy to private conversations between myself and close friends and family. A visit to my cell phone retailer revealed software had been installed, enabling anyone to listen to my personal phone calls, view my address book, and read my text messages. This witness was to testify on my behalf, but was sent home by my attorney before taking the stand. Ms. Esposito was later heard on tape giving detailed instructions on how to use GPS devices to track me and Chad. I placed an infrared camera outside my home and caught Nick on my property numerous times, including seeing his facial impression on the glass of my back door.

Everywhere I went I saw him. Either that or he would send me a text to let me know he knew every move I was making. It was obvious he wanted me to know what he was doing, and it was terrifying. In an attempt to shake him, I would change my routine or take different routes to work. Despite my best efforts, his eyes were everywhere. With the start of each new day, I was becoming more and more of a nervous wreck. Nowhere I went was safe; I was constantly looking over my shoulder. My security had been breached, my privacy violated, and the once secure, fun, outgoing Jennie was gone. In her place was a woman trapped in her own home, fearful and suspicious of the outside world. My cries to law enforcement continued to go unanswered, and I began to feel as though I had nowhere to turn.

While we hear so much about stalking and the violence that often ensues from these situations, I think, like so much in our society, we've been desensitized to just how dangerous it is for the victims who suffer from it. There have been countless books, movies, television shows, and news stories dedicated to the subject, yet I still think some people don't believe it's a valid issue.

Part of the problem, I believe, lies in the somewhat misguided stereotype of stalkers that has pervaded our society. I think there is a widely held belief that stalkers are crazed boogeymen who lurk unseen in the shadows, or that victims are only famous people. According to an American National Violence Against Women Survey, eight percent of women report being stalked in their lifetime and are overwhelmingly stalked by former romantic partners. (Although you can be stalked by casual acquaintances or coworkers, for the most part women experience this trauma at the hands of those who know them best and most intimately—former lovers.) Women are also ten times more likely to be physically assaulted by their stalkers.

Experts agree that stalking behaviors are willful and malicious, provoke fear and discomfort, are invasive, and are directed at one person on an ongoing basis. The most common behaviors associated with stalking are repeated phone calls, sometimes threatening in nature, surveillance, and repeated unwanted contact. According to several psychological studies, once a stalker feels as though he's been "abandoned," he will tap into all the tools he has in his arsenal, including economic abuse, recurrent litigation, verbal and psychological abuse, and physical coercion. Another method stalkers use to get to you is triangulation, or striking out at the things or people that matter to you, such as close friends and family, and, of course, the new partner you choose to move on with.

What complicated my situation was the fact that Nick and I had just gone through a high-conflict divorce. When it comes to matters of marriage, many people choose to stay uninvolved, deeming what goes on between a husband and wife is none of their concern. What's worse is that your spouse knows you like no one else; he can turn on you with stone-cold viciousness that leaves you reeling. Much like stalking, the high-conflict divorce becomes a high-stakes battle. According the Minnesota Center Against Violence and Abuse, "Virtually all coverage of a high-conflict divorce assumes both parents are the source of the conflict...blame is assigned solely and equally to the parents in essentially all cases without much analysis. However, if one party is abusive and sufficiently wealthy to fund on-going litigation, the Domestic Court may be ideally suited to the spurned mate's agenda." This essentially gives the person with the biggest bank account free rein to plunder your life and bring you to your knees—it becomes sanctioned by the court system!

There are many similarities between an abusive relationship and a high-conflict divorce. The power of the abuser is transferred to the professionals, and worse it is perfectly legal. The center terms high-conflict divorce as a:

> "manifestation of stalking behaviors by wealthy domestic abusers… [F]amily court lends itself to use as a forum for post-separation stalking… [E]xperts who write about high-conflict divorce describe the same findings as the experts who write about stalkers and batterers, but lay blame equally on both parties, citing interparental conflict as the problem. In describing interparental conflict, authors cite physical assault, stalking, economic abuse, verbal and psychological abuse, physical coercion, and recurrent litigation. Individuals in high-conflict divorces are alternately enraged and deeply emotionally injured by the actions of their ex-spouse."

It makes my blood run cold to think the justice system can be party to the further abuse of the very people it is supposed to protect. Why has no one stood up for the countless victims of this endless cycle of abuse? Why has this system of "justice" been allowed to continue unchallenged? Why are abusers given the right to abuse?

Nick was quite crafty in the way he played the legal system, for he did all of these things and more to me—and there was nothing I could do about it. He twisted and turned the system to his advantage, being proactive in his actions, leaving me on the offensive, scrambling to play catch-up. In spite of all the evidence I had to prove the torture he was putting me through, I was never able to receive my protective orders. Like most stalkers Nick wasn't stupid—he knew how to play the system to his advantage. While he was fairly blatant in his campaign against me, most stalkers won't make actual written or verbal threats against their victims. However, they will send enough messages to let you know loud and clear their intent against you. It might be a dead animal on your front porch, threatening notes disguised as love letters, or sending you dead flowers. I once received the "gift" of a live snake coiled inside a bowl that was loosely covered by foil in my kitchen. This can go on for years, and nothing will ever be done to the people who do things like this.

Being stalked by a former partner is considered the most dangerous type of stalking in existence. It tends to last longer and be more intense—and more violent. Another study found that 50 to 60 percent of women have been physically abused by their stalkers, either during the relationship or right after the breakup occurred, and often the violence begins before the relationship even ends. The physical and emotional abuse, shocking actions (such as leaving dead animals for you), and surveillance are all strong indicators of extreme violence.

Stalkers often exhibit problems maintaining stable connections and normal relationships, and typically don't have social skills or empathy for the feelings of others. They vacillate between deep devotion and bitter rejection, and usually have low self-esteem. Many stalkers are found to have narcissistic, borderline, histrionic, or antisocial personality disorder as well as schizophrenia and depression. As a result of the ongoing stalking, the victim will suffer long-term psychological stress including headaches, trouble sleeping, depression, anxiety, and trouble concentrating.

In my case, as my court battles raged on and Nick's stalking continued, I became physically ill. I eventually had to be admitted to a hospital for excessive vomiting, bleeding ulcers, and high blood pressure. I felt like I was being sucked into a vortex every day. I had nothing to anchor myself to in order to keep from being annihilated by this gaping maw that was pulling me under. I lived in abject fear that if I let my guard down for even a second, Nick would turn the full force of his rage on me, which I knew would be worse than anything he'd done to me so far.

My life was on the line, and I felt the only way to protect myself was to have a male friend stay with me. I had met a man by the name of Chad, and we'd become friends. I shared with him all the upheaval I was being subjected to courtesy of Nick, and he promised to help me and protect me. It put my mind at ease knowing I had some measure of defense against Nick's machinations, and I hoped this would decrease the tension in my life.

It enraged Nick to learn I had male company (platonic though it was). By that point I was terrified to be alone, open

prey to Nick and his continued campaign of terror against
me. I didn't want to leave the house because I was mistrustful
of what Nick might do, and therefore I became a hostage in
my own home. For a brief moment, in my desperation to end
this nightmare I attempted to reconcile with Nick. Unfortunately, this backfired. It only caused more strife in the home
and let loose a whole new torrent of threats. He warned me
that calling the police would be futile, and promised again
and again he would have my children taken away from me.
Whenever his tirades began, I would resort to calling a girlfriend or my mother so they could hear his rants against me.
After a few months of this, I was finally able to get him out of
my home, but the damage was done. My children and I were
stressed out beyond belief, and it didn't appear there would
be an end to the nightmare.

I was admitted to the hospital a second time for a sur-
gical endoscopy to assess the damage being done to my body
due to the high amount of stress I was under. My heart rate
elevated to such a high level, a cardiologist was called in to
stabilize me. At that point I had resumed my relationship
with Chad, eventually requesting that he stay over in order
to keep Nick out.

On the morning of my surgery, Nick came to the house
at 7:30 to bang on the door and yell for me to come out. I was
ill and couldn't do much, so Chad did his best to persuade
Nick to leave. He tried to appeal to Nick's rational side by
reminding Nick he was scaring the children with his tirades,
bringing them to tears. Nick's response was to yell that he

and Tommy were protecting their kids, and if I called the cops they were all going to have a "powwow" down the road.

Nick even sent his father to my home at 8:00 a.m. to bang on my door, knowing a man was staying in my home (this happened on multiple occasions, including the morning of Valentine's Day). When that did not work, he would send texts to my parents about me, as if he could somehow shame me into no longer having a man stay with me overnight. Finally, in retaliation for what he saw as my betrayal for having male company in my home, Nick slapped me with an injunction, barring me from having any men in my home past 8:00 p.m. This was a classic case of Nick using the judicial system against me to further his own agenda.

Nick kept me tied up in court with yet more motions to prevent me from seeing Chad. He began to come into my home again, ignoring my repeated requests that he leave, indicating he would do so when he was "good and ready." I resorted to having someone at home with me whenever Nick would come by to pick up Hunter. However, this was a strain for me, as I didn't have many friends left because of Nick, and the ones I did have had their own lives to tend to; they didn't have time to babysit me. When I had a friend over and he or she answered the door, Nick would demand to see me, and if I didn't come to the door he would leave only to come back a few minutes later. Eventually I would be so worn out I would come to the door just to get him to leave for good.

I was frantic for a solution, and I asked my attorney, Kent Shriver, what course of action was available to me. He advised me to marry Chad, which meant Nick would not be able to bar him from my house, thus providing me with a measure of protection. It wasn't a perfect solution, but it was the only feasible one available to me. I proposed the idea to Chad, and he agreed to go along with it. More than anything I hoped this arrangement would give me some peace. By then that was what I wanted—just to have a little bit of peace in my life. I fully admit my main motivation for taking a husband was to shield myself against Nick and his volatility. Some might say there were other options; however, when you're faced with a dangerous situation such as my children and I were, you will do almost anything to protect yourself.

Chad's presence in my life did not provide the respite I had hoped for. If anything it ignited Nick into coming after me with both barrels. He filed to secure full custody of Hunter, allowing me only scant visitation. Going after me wasn't enough for Nick; he turned the full force of his fury on Chad, seeking to eliminate him from my life. Chad was fired from two jobs, and physically assaulted twice by Nick. We called the police, who did nothing except add to my family's emotional turmoil. Nick resurrected one of his former tricks by digging into his own chest to produce a red mark, so he could claim Chad had assaulted him. However, there were several witnesses who saw Nick walk into our backyard, and it was only after he was asked to leave that he pushed Chad.

I also discovered later that much in the same way he had teamed up with Tommy against me, Nick had recruited Chad's ex-wife to be a soldier in this war. Whereas Chad and his ex-wife had coexisted, once Nick interfered she began to harass Chad incessantly, and even instigated a nasty court battle to reverse the custody order for their children, keeping him tied up with costly and time-consuming hearings, motions, and trials.

Eventually Nick was able to use Chad as the ultimate weapon against me in our own ongoing custody clashes. As one of his legal maneuvers, Nick insisted both Chad and I undergo a battery of drug tests. Even though we passed with flying colors, Nick wasn't satisfied. He and Tommy were granted motions to depose Chad's parents, and eventually succeeded in forcing us to submit to a second round of testing. Every move Nick made in court, Tommy was sure to follow. I begged Mr. Shriver to intervene; his response was to ask for another $15,000 or he would resign from my case. I didn't have it, and was forced to seek other counsel. Not trusting anyone in Montgomery County, I hired a Houston attorney.

Initially it seemed I had made the right decision. Bert Steinmann was appointed as an amicus (an objective individual who relays his observations about the home environment and interactions with the child to the court) for Aidan, while Hunter was assigned to undergo a social study conducted by Attorney Laura Maulberger. My hopes were soon dashed, as most motions my new attorney filed were repeatedly denied. I was unable to connect with either of these court-appointed attorneys after countless attempts and many long months. My new attorney was shocked by what was going on, though for me it was starting to feel like every other day of my life since this nightmare started.

Chad balked at being asked to go through another hair follicle drug test, and refused. Although I explained the importance of complying with the judge's orders, he refused, saying he could no longer continue to live this way. While I couldn't blame him for his refusal, I also recognized he was sacrificing my children and me in the process. Chad abandoned our family that day; I was left with no choice but to file for divorce, cutting him out of my life.

It wasn't until much later that I learned Chad had been complicit with Tommy. Some in my life believe Nick and/or Tommy paid him off to insinuate himself into my life, therefore giving them more ammunition in their custody battles against me. I did come across evidence that Chad was paid upward of $70,000 by one of my exes, and that one of Nick's neighbors could be heard bragging about Chad being sent out of town by the co-conspirators. I've not talked to Chad since our divorce, and he wasn't present during the trials, so I don't know how much validity there is to these claims. However, considering how he sacrificed my children and me, I have to wonder if there was a kernel of truth behind the rumors around town. I attempted to prove in court how the men continually teamed up against me, but to no avail.

Unbelievably, my mother proved to be my rock throughout this entire ordeal. We had begun to talk daily, up to three times a day, and she witnessed firsthand Nick's brutality toward me. She knew he hadn't been a proper husband to me, that he'd never contributed anything to our household and always put his buddies ahead of our family. Many times during the marriage, whenever she and I would talk on the phone, Nick would hover over me, demanding I hang up immediately. On several occasions she even reached out to Nick's father to voice concern over his son's behavior, recording the calls and the father's blasé attitude about Nick's actions. She knew how I bent over backward to try to keep the peace with Nick and Tommy, all for the good of my children. It was amazing to me that my mother and I had come to this place of love, hope, and respect on our journey. I couldn't love her more if I tried, and I'm proud to call her my mom.

CHAPTER 8

After All

After months of attempts on my part to get in touch with Mr. Steinmann and Ms. Maulberger, a month before my trials were to begin they called me.

Mr. Steinmann visited my home for a few moments, and led me to believe there were no problems. In fact he submitted an order to the court recommending Tommy's child support payments for Aidan be increased to the maximum. He asked me to contact him regarding Nick's episodes and Tommy's refusal to follow court orders. Although I followed his advice and called him, I only got his voicemail, and once again left several messages that were not returned. The next contact I received from Mr. Steinmann was through my attorney, stating I owed him $10,000.

Ms. Maulberger informed she'd visited the Mortons on

multiple occasions. However, I only spoke with her for fifteen minutes before she rushed out of town for the holidays. According to her, I owed her $3,000 for the evaluation. Neither Mr. Steinmann nor Ms. Maulberger contacted any of my witnesses nor spent any length of time with me or my family. My attorney told me not to worry, as my reputation was above reproach and I was an excellent mother.

My trial with Nick was first, and to the surprise of my attorney and me, Mr. Steinmann testified in Hunter's trial, though he had no involvement with the case. He recommended Aidan stay with Tommy, while Ms. Maulberger stated Hunter would be better off with Nick. According to her, when she compared notes with Mr. Steinmann, they found "inconsistencies" in my story revolving around the children's bedrooms. The blood drained from my cheeks in shock. How could this be happening? I was being called a liar in open court, and to rub salt into the wound they were obviously working together—without any truth to their claims—to railroad me.

When it came time for my attorney to cross-examine them, he shredded their testimony and, backed up by my evidence, proved perjury on both their parts. He also uncovered that before my divorce was final Nick had acquired $950,000, which I had no knowledge of, and he had altered evidence. However, neither suffered consequences for their actions, and my disheartened attorney fled Montgomery County, saying his own actions had made it impossible for him to practice there. He hasn't been back since.

Nick and Tommy finally emerged triumphant against me, and in 2011 I lost custody of Hunter, and the next week Aidan.

I was allowed to see Hunter on the second, fourth, and fifth weekends of the month, as well as every other holiday; I was granted visitation with Aidan on the second and fourth weekends of each month.

I cannot adequately describe the trauma of having your young children ripped away from you. I did everything for my children, keeping them busy with activities, providing them with a beautiful home, and keeping them clean and well fed. When I knew I was going to be the single mother of two boys who would be about the same age, I felt it was important they be raised together and have each other to lean on. Knowing that not only would they be ripped away from me but from each other was equally devastating.

It is not an exaggeration for me to say I was at my lowest point. The only outcome I'd ever envisioned when this nightmare began was that Hunter and Aidan would remain with me while I co-parented with Nick and Tommy, as that was what was best for all of us. How a judge could see it any other way was beyond my comprehension.

The constant court appearances, attorneys' fees, mental evaluations, and drug tests I was required to undergo cost me close to $200,000. In addition to the financial hit, I lost my job, which impacted my ability to recoup my losses. In fighting these custody battles, I had gone through my entire savings and was forced to empty out my 401(k) account, putting my financial future in further jeopardy. Even as my life was swirling down the tubes, it wasn't enough for Nick. He continued to stalk me, and his family kept up their smear tactics, further dragging my name through the mud.

It was only one week after losing custody that I was served with yet another court appearance order from Tommy and then one from Nick. I made the brutal decision to sell my beautiful house and leave Montgomery County. The mandate by Chuck that I stay there to give him access to Kaytlin was no longer valid, as he had all but turned his back on her, seeing her sporadically at most. While Hunter and Aidan were there, nothing else kept me there. I needed to escape from the madness swirling around me; I couldn't see any other way for me to regain my sanity and regroup well enough to get my kids back.

At this extremely low period in my life, I needed people around me I could trust, people I could confide in. Because of Nick's machinations, I had lost many close friends, either because he'd kept me isolated from them during our marriage, or because they'd suffered devastating consequences at his hands, including job losses and lawsuits. I felt quite alone in the world.

Being in my thirties and going through my fourth divorce was certainly not the way I had seen my life unfolding. I was a smart woman in so many aspects of my life; I'd always worked hard, followed the right path, and made sound career moves, allowing me to create a comfortable life for me and my children. I made a vow that I would focus on me and put romance on the back burner.

When I made the decision to sell my house, I began the process of getting it ready for market. There were several improvements that needed to be made, but because of my financial situation I was wary about how much the repairs would cost. I believe God sends people into our lives for a reason, and it was at this point He sent me someone who would not only help me with my home but provide the shoulder I desperately needed.

I found Chad (not to be confused with my ex-husband Chad) when I went online to try to find someone to assist me with the restoration work I needed done on my house. I'd been quoted extremely high prices, and I was distressed that I would not be able to afford the work I needed done, and therefore would take a huge loss when I sold the house. God sent me an angel in the form of Chad, who agreed to do the work for free, charging me only for the materials. I was so grateful for his generosity. It restored the faith I had lost in people, reminding me all over again there are good people in the world.

As Chad worked on my house, we became friendly, and just by being around him I could tell he had a good heart and a kind, open spirit. I also discovered we were both strong in our faith, believing in the almighty presence of God in our everyday lives. As I believe in the power of positivity, I would text him little inspirational quotes throughout the day to provide a bright spot for him. He let me know how much he appreciated the gesture, and it wasn't long before we were talking on the phone on a daily basis, followed by casual lunches and dinners. We became good friends in a very short amount of time.

Though Chad and I weren't in a romantic relationship, I felt as though I could trust him completely with the details of my life. I also thought it was only fair that if he were going to be in my life, I let him know right away about my immediate past and what he could potentially be dealing with as a result of being friends with me. I poured my heart out to him, telling him about the relationships with Tommy and Nick, the marriage, the stalking, the harassment, and the custody battles. I know he initially thought everything I told him was preposterous, and he took it with a grain of salt. However, in spite of his skepticism, he remained my friend, offering me his support, his ear, and, most valuable of all, his trust whenever I needed it.

As our conversations continued, Chad and I indeed became closer, and our feelings turned romantic. He was one of the sweetest, most caring people I'd ever met. The difference this time was I went into the relationship with my eyes wide open. I could already feel a definitive shift in my thinking with regard to relationships and men, and for the first time I stopped to listen for the whispers.

There weren't any.

Though I was happier than I had been in a long time, I was also fearful of the potential retaliation against me as well as him if we continued the relationship. I warned Chad that anyone who'd been involved with me, romantically or otherwise, had been fired from their jobs, forced into court, and stalked and harassed. He assured me he wasn't afraid, and because he owned his own business was confident in the knowledge that nothing could harm the sterling reputation he'd built for himself in the area. He could count several high-profile individuals in the Houston area, including professional athletes and NASA astronauts, as longtime clients, and was secure in those relationships.

I tried to be as certain as Chad, but history had taught me never to underestimate Nick's wrath. However, it wasn't long before my predictions came true.

By then Chad and I were spending much of our time with each other. It gave me comfort and security to have him around the house as Nick's reign of terror continued with constant stalking and harassment. Once Nick realized Chad and I were becoming close, the campaign against him began. The first grenade Nick threw was injunctions barring Chad from being around Hunter. The second offensive occurred when Nick texted to say he had received a phone call from a man claiming Chad owed him a large sum of money. Suspicious about this call, and familiar with the type of intimidation tactics Nick would use, Chad contacted Nick directly. Nick proceeded to badmouth me, and warned Chad to stay away from me.

After further investigation Chad discovered that Nick had coerced his ex-girlfriend's father (and the mother of his son) into fabricating the existence of this debt, and worse convinced him to put liens against all of his customers. Being followed around town by private detectives hired by Nick had become an unfortunate fact of my life, and Chad was no exception. His ten-year-old daughter, Piper, had even begun to notice we were being tailed, including a mysterious car that followed us all day and night.

For the sake of their child, Chad had maintained a peaceful relationship with his ex-girlfriend and, by extension, her father, a successful businessman. Nick's special talent is hitting people where it will hurt them the most, and in this case he went after Chad's livelihood and business reputation.

The liens against Chad's customers began to pile up, which in turn impacted other areas of his finances. A deal he had in the works to buy an apartment building fell through, and one by one longtime vendors started to drop his business. I predicted it wouldn't be long before Chad's ex-girlfriend would join the fray, but he didn't want to believe she would get involved, as it was not her way to allow herself to be drawn into this type of situation. I knew better; if it meant punishing me, Nick and Tommy would pull her into it.

Unfortunately, my predictions were borne out. Once she discovered Chad and I were dating, she turned on him and, ultimately, me. As the injunctions against me concerning Chad continued, she testified on behalf of Nick and Tommy, telling outrageous lies that were totally unfounded about Chad's behavior and actions. She was quite convincing. When Chad testified on my behalf, Nick and Tommy's attorneys tried every dirty, underhanded trick in the book to try to make it seem as if Chad were up to no good, including insinuating he'd done several long-term stints in prison, and forcing him to reveal private information about himself in order to save his credibility. Although he was able to discredit some of the damaging testimony from his ex, it didn't carry enough weight, and he was made to look like a fool, which ultimately meant he could not be around my children.

Finally, I could take it no more and decided it was time for me to go into seclusion. I packed up my belongings and left my house, deciding to let my real estate agent handle the sale. My peace of mind had been completely shattered, and now someone else I cared for so deeply was being made to pay the price for being in my life. I needed to escape sooner rather than later.

I was forced to live like a vagrant. Chad, Kaytlin, Piper, and I moved into an extended-stay hotel for a month, and this was when I decided I needed to let Tommy and Nick know I wanted to get settled for at least a month before picking up the boys. We were hesitant to commit to buying or even leasing anything since we had no way of knowing from one day to the next what might happen to us. During that time we felt relatively safe. However, within two weeks Chad's business accounts were frozen (fraudulently), and after completion of a lucrative job he was stiffed his $7,000 fee. Worse, we returned from my uncle's funeral to discover Chad's ex had taken his truck, and we later learned from the front office staff that several people had come by to inquire about me specifically. Once again safety and vulnerability became most prominent in our minds. However, with money running low, we needed to find an alternative, so after a month Chad's brother took us into his home.

After we made the transition we were discovered, and the stalking began again. Neighbors reported to us that they saw strange people loitering outside the building at all hours of the day and night. The worst moment came when the house was broken into; the doors were propped open, and items were shifted around. Whoever had broken in wanted us to know they'd been there, and wanted to send us a message. I also knew I was being watched, as I often saw various vehicles following me.

By then I was nearly catatonic. Nick had indeed broken me. I ceased to be a functioning human being, and, in fear of my life, I finally knuckled under to the pressure cooker I was in. I refused to step foot outside the bedroom. I locked myself in there for six weeks, unable to live my life, which included performing my job. Though my supervisor was already aware of my legal issues, I reached out to him to let him know I could not continue to work in Houston, and asked for a transfer to another city in the state. A position had opened up in Georgia, and though I was reluctant to move so far away from my children, out of loyalty to the company I decided to pursue the opportunity. However, as I went through the interview process, I continued to be slapped with lawsuits. I just gave up. I simply didn't have it in me to keep moving forward, and went to my supervisor and let him know I would not be continuing with the process. He wanted to work with me, but I could see he was weary of dealing with this situation. I was given one week to reconsider my position on the matter, and rather than fire me he allowed me to resign. I was devastated beyond belief. This was such a great job; it had given me and my children so many unbelievable opportunities. Yet one more victory for Nick in his crusade to destroy me.

Out of money and, quite honestly, feeling completely out of hope, once again I had to move home with my family while I tried to regroup. I had been drained emotionally, spiritually, physically, and financially, and in the end I had nothing to show for it.

Although I did not pursue the job opportunity, I still decided I would need to leave the Houston area altogether. I wanted to be near my family. I needed to draw strength from them. I needed to heal, and I knew the only way I would be able to do that was if I cocooned myself in their love and support.

Chad, Kaytlin, Piper, and I packed up once more, put our belongings in storage, and moved home to Athens. I felt like such an utter failure. I had been a happy, successful, and independent woman. Yet again I was at a terrible crossroads in my life, and I had to face up to the fact that I had played a hand in my misfortune. It was a bitter pill to swallow, but if I was going to move forward with my life I would have to accept that harsh truth.

Living in Athens with my parents put an inevitable strain

on my relationship with Chad. He'd been forced to give up his home in Houston and dismantle his business, and find his clients new vendors to work with. Starting over in a new city was tough for him, as he didn't have the reputation or contacts, and the two-hour drive from Athens to Dallas made it nearly impossible for him to operate a business.

The final straw came when Chad took a job at an Air Force base, which required a background check. An outstanding DUI warrant (for which he'd already served his thirty days and paid $6,000 in fines) turned up; the warrant had been reissued a mere week after he had testified in Tommy's and Nick's trials, and he was arrested immediately. The bail was set at an astronomical rate, so high we couldn't even come up with the requisite ten percent. He was forced to sit in jail for three days while awaiting extradition back to Oklahoma, the state of the original warrant. Eventually he put items of expensive machinery related to his business up for collateral, and he was released.

I drove him immediately to Oklahoma in order to get this straightened out, and to my surprise, after going to the city clerk's office, the district clerk's office, the DA's office, and even the judge's chamber, we found there was not an active warrant. Even though neither of us said it, we knew someone acting on Nick's behalf had to be behind it, but we couldn't prove it. After much investigation and legal wrangling, Chad was able to get it taken care of, but it was too late. The financial damage was done.

The mental, emotional, and financial strain of trying to

resurrect his career from the ashes, coupled with the arrest, was too much; Chad and I decided to end our romantic relationship. We knew we'd always love each other, but it had become too difficult to try to stay together. Although we parted ways, I knew Chad would never be out of my life completely, and some part of me even held the belief that we would be together again one day.

Being back in the Dallas area, about a four-hour drive from Montgomery County, meant I would have to make the trip back to Houston to see my boys. Tommy and Nick refused to meet me even at a halfway point between our two cities, meaning I logged two eight-hour drives three weekends a month. In a particularly gut-wrenching twist, my custody agreement with Tommy dictated that my mother accompany me on the trips; otherwise Aidan would not be handed over to me. Strangely enough this particular injunction was typed up by Nick's attorney, Ms. Esposito. Furthermore my signature was forged on this document. It was only when I traveled to Houston (without my mother, who was too sick to come with me) to pick up Aidan that I learned about this latest legal maneuver. Tommy and Nick were both well aware of my mother's declining health and inability to take long trips. Not only was I being made to suffer, but my mother was also being told she would have to make a sacrifice as well. As she became sicker and unable to make the trip, I would miss out on my visitation with Aidan, and my sons would miss out on time with each other.

Even though they had ground me into dust, Nick and

Tommy remained determined to keep putting me through the wringer. Chad and I remained in contact, and he called to warn me his ex-girlfriend had informed him that Nick knew an old boyfriend from high school had reached out to me. She also mentioned that Nick's attorney had advised her of what testimony she should give during the trials, and how to track Chad in order to find one or both of us.

Perhaps their sickest violation against me was when they conspired to keep Aidan and Hunter away from me on Mother's Day, which fell on my normal day of visitation. They knew I couldn't be two places at once, yet strategically arranged to have Aidan and Hunter in two opposing locations, preventing me from collecting my boys. They constantly compared notes about how they could keep me jumping through their hoops. Tommy was frequently keeping Aidan away from me, costing me time with my son, and Nick tried to get me to pay the maximum amount of child support as well as his legal fees. While I am required to pay Nick the upper limit of child support, the judge, perhaps feeling slightly remorseful, denied Nick's request that I pay his attorney's fees (though I did get stuck paying some of Tommy's legal fees). When I filed a bill of review on the final orders in Judge Hamilton's court, I found a portion of the order to which I had not agreed. It also contained my forged signature. In addition I asked to vacate the orders Judge Hamilton signed after the temporary order trial. This was when I learned about recusals. To recuse is to remove yourself voluntarily from a case to avoid impropriety. In this instance Judge Hamilton recused herself from my custody trial, as she knew the Mortons. However, she reinstated herself one week later to sign a restraining order against me, preventing me from seeing my son Aidan, and to oversee a trial being brought against me by Tommy.

I was continually portrayed as the bad parent. Every decision I'd made in my life was turned against me, and innocent actions were blown out of proportion. While every custody case is different, and is comprised of its own intricacies such as child abuse, therefore requiring alternative decisions, under no circumstance should a child ever be used as a weapon against the other parent.

My exes and their attorneys twisted my decision to have children out of wedlock, painting me as promiscuous and condemning me for my bad choices, i.e. my children. However, my children are the BEST choices I've ever made. They are gifts from God, and I chose to bring them into this world out of love and an unselfish desire to provide them with the best lives I could. My four marriages had been disparaged, yet no one can deny I always provided for my children. They had the best of everything, and there has never been a time in their lives when they felt there wasn't anything I couldn't give to them. If anything I made bad choices in men, though I cannot control another person's actions. However, I do make the choice that I will not continue to allow bad behavior, as it taints my life and the lives of my children. I choose instead to ensure my family unit is safe, and will place the needs of my children above the needs of an abusive partner.

My decision to take my children to counseling was also disparaged. The reason I chose to take my children to counseling was to ensure they weren't suffering any ill effects from the negativity swirling around us. I wanted to make sure they were okay, and to equip them with the coping skills they needed to help them deal with the negative situation they'd been thrust into.

I had to search deep within myself to find out what values are most important to me, and after much self-discovery I now know what my five core values are: responsibility, integrity, loyalty, achievement, and discipline. Had I been more in tune with them, I would have made different choices. However, I know I will stick to them as I continue into my future.

Knowing what I know now, are there different decisions I would have made? Absolutely. Of course, as the old saying goes, hindsight is 20/20. No one is perfect, and we will all stumble in this life before we leave it. By knowing the core YOU, you can use your own personal values to guide you to the right path and make decisions based on sound intuition and knowledge, not fear and uncertainty.

It's true when they say love is blind. I juggled thoughts of leaving in order to protect my children and staying to keep the family structure intact. Either decision had tragic consequences. I just wanted everyone to get along and be able to move forward in a positive manner. I was stalked, battered, harassed, and ganged up on by my exes before being brought to the brink of emotional and financial devastation. I searched for answers as to how this could have happened to me and discovered a phenomenon known as *abuse by proxy*, a common tactic among narcissists in which they use others to do their dirty work. They recruit friends, family members, institutions, and authorities to do their bidding, crafting scenarios designed to humiliate and embarrass. They coerce, threaten, stalk, harass, convince, and tempt others into going along with their sinister plans. These people are but mere means to an end for the person who uses abuse by proxy. Nick perpetuated this upon me in spades.

I cannot understand how engaging in these behaviors could be considered productive, particularly as the party being portrayed as the bad parent is the one being placed under the magnifying glass. As I look back, I see I was walking on eggshells most of the time. I tried to comply with everyone else's wishes in order to make them happy, and by giving up control over my own life I allowed others to define me physically and emotionally, making it impossible for me to function. I bent over backward to implement the requests of the court and my exes for the sake of my children. However, it was not humanly impossible for me to do it by myself—I needed the cooperation of my sons' fathers to make it happen. Sadly, they weren't interested in the welfare of the children. It was more important to torture me, and to do everything in their power to make me suffer. I continued to ask myself how any of it was useful, as it cost me financially and emotionally, and worst of all resulted in the loss of my children. How did *any* of this benefit my children?

Being dragged through the mud by Tommy and Nick was a detriment to my overall well-being, which impacted the emotional health of my children. I jumped through every hoop imaginable to give 110 percent: I took my kids to counselors and doctors, and I attended parenting classes in addition to my own personal life-coaching sessions. I ensured Kaytlin had top-notch tutoring, and she and Aidan participated in extracurricular and school activities such as dance, soccer, baseball, volleyball, volunteer activities, band, and Bible school. I met with my daughter's teachers on a regular basis to check on her progress and establish open communication between all of us.

This was in addition to attending depositions, meeting with my attorneys, and attending scheduled court dates, which turned out to be a huge waste of time—many days I would rush to make it to court at the appointed time only to sit for four hours, waiting to be called, and in the end have my court date rescheduled. Even in the midst of the hurricane that had become my life, I still had to successfully maintain my full-time job, something that was becoming harder to do as time went on.

I know all of this was the fulfillment of Nick's promise to break me, an attempt to bring me down and cause me to fail, versus operating in the best interest of the children. Nick and Tommy manipulated the court system, turning it into a long arm of abuse against me. There was no room for me or my children to fit any more court-compelled motions into our lives. Nick and Tommy wanted to keep me from being a successful mother. Many times I wanted to say to the judge, "This is what I do. What do they do?" Were they representing a progressive, positive parenting environment that revolved around fostering their children's success? Were they shielding their children from the harmful effects of constant litigation? Were they putting aside their negative feelings toward me and directing positive energy toward their children? No! They were doing the exact opposite! The arrows clearly pointed to every action and reaction being about *their* interests versus the *children's* interests!

Throughout this entire ordeal, my number one concern was the emotional, physical, and financial well-being of my children. I couldn't help but feel as though I was the only one with this goal. It seemed their fathers were concerned with bringing me down. I did everything the courts, counselors, doctors, and Nick and Tommy requested, and more. I dotted all I's and crossed all T's. It was time for me to stand up and be in charge. I wanted the fathers of my children to step up to the plate and truly serve the children's needs instead of their own.

As long as they were calling the shots, I would not get my desired outcome, which was to put a stop to the emotional abuse of my children. That meant no more court motions, lawsuits, and restraining orders. I let them control the situation and twist and turn it to their advantage. I knew the time had come for me to shine a light on their actions and showcase how I had been proactive by taking parenting classes and seeking counselors for my children. I had done everything I could to minimize the damage to my children. Their fathers had done nothing, but inflict emotional harm upon them. I couldn't understand why we couldn't all work together for and engage in actions that were in the best interests of the children. Didn't that make the most sense?

I began to reach out to various individuals and support groups to help me advocate for my children, making it clear I was willing to do all the work. What I found was alarming. These types of groups either did not exist or were under attack by political groups, and had been forced to disband or go underground for fear of retribution. I continued to root myself in the belief that goodwill produces a great wall of protection around the one who sends it, and no weapon that is formed against him or her shall prosper.

I know this sounds hard to believe, but in spite of everything I prayed for my exes and their families to find peace in their own lives—and I continue to do so to this day. When negative thoughts invaded my space, I came up with a process to help me combat their power over me—something I like to call the three R's: **recognize** the negative thought, **reject** that negative thought, and **reorganize** it into a positive thought. It was a daily, conscious thought of mine to radiate positivity, and to have it reflect in everything I did with work, my kids, even strangers I met.

Many believe it takes twenty-one days to reorganize your brain's thought patterns. It took a lot of hard work on my part to remind myself every day to practice this mantra, especially as I was drowning in negativity. However, the payoff in the long run was extraordinary; my children's emotional health improved, as they were being raised in a positive environment and shielded from all the muck I was wading through. I was striving for success in my outlook in life, and I achieved it. I realize to some people it may sound silly to practice daily affirmations, but I swear by their power. In the beginning I repeated these affirmations to myself, almost like a chant, until they became as natural to me as taking a breath. I would leave inspiring notes to my children on the bathroom mirror, and it became such a life-affirming ritual that each morning when they woke up they would rush to the mirror to see what message Mom had for them that day. I made it a point that as we sat down to dinner each evening, I would go around the table and ask each child (little ones included), "What did you contribute to the world today?" This worked two-fold; over time, the children began to understand they were expected to produce an important contribution to the dinner table conversation, which involved their being valued and accepted on a number of levels. Second, it inspired them to go out into the world each and every day to look for little ways they could help others, or give something to the world around them. We are all a part of this world, and we all must contribute, so therefore I chose to represent positive reinforcement to my children and to those around me. I chose to kick the "committee" to the curb, i.e. my exes, their families, and any other individual who I allowed to create misery in my life. In essence, I told them, "Thank you for coming, however it is time go, because the party is over." I chose to overcome the adversity in my life, and fill it with success. I chose not be a victim. I chose to be empowered.

Many thought it was my end, to which I say, "No. It has actually just begun."

CHAPTER 9

Learning the Lessons

Looking back now, I can see the path that led me to this point. I didn't listen to the whispers. I spent too much time bending over backward to please others to the detriment of myself, and ultimately my children. I had falsely held fast to the belief that others in the world were "good people," as I have always considered myself to be, and would never intentionally set out to hurt another human being. I underestimated the greed and innate evil of others, and as a result I paid the highest-price possible. I began to look inward to try to figure out how to reset my personal course, to determine a new path for myself so that I would never again tune out my intuition. Your intuition will never mislead you. It's when we go against it that we find ourselves in dire straits.

I was battle-scarred from dealing with Nick, Tommy, and the corruption within the county. I felt as though I couldn't sink any lower in my life. All of my accomplishments, all of the heights I'd scaled and conquered, had been diminished to the tiniest grains of sand. When I lost custody, it would have been akin to the judge pulling out a gun and shooting me himself. I truly wanted to crawl under a rock and take the abuse that had been heaped upon me, because I had honestly believed I would never crawl up from the abyss I'd been thrown into.

However, it's when we are at our lowest points that we must retreat and regroup to find our strength anew. I knew they wanted to keep me down, and make me believe that I deserved what they had thrown at me. These were some of my darkest days, and I had to fight my way back toward the light in order to emerge stronger and more determined than ever.

It is always darkest before the dawn.

After I made a vow to myself that I would take control of my life by developing a new philosophy of life and mission statement for myself, I wrote a mantra that I committed to memory and would put into practice each and every day of my life:

Jennie's Operating Philosophy of Life and Mission Statement

I, Jennie, am dedicated to self-mastery and achievement. I will continually learn in order to achieve self-excellence, and my commitment to high quality performance produces outstanding results of lasting value. My faithfulness to this commitment resonates within my family/organizations, and is expressed in every area of my life...physically, mentally, emotionally, spirituality, and financially.

My work and social life reflect my values of integrity, responsibility, loyalty, discipline, and achievement.

I use my persistence, determination, dynamic personality, and creativity to exert influence with others. Experience, confidence, ability to acquire knowledge, and resilience are my strongest personal resources, and I use them to excel and achieve any given task as a talented inspirational leader—personally and professionally.

I am recognized for being exceptional at everything that I do; powerfully motivating, and persistent in seeing that every achievement is unsurpassed. Prestige, integrity, and an ethic of excellence surround every facet of my life. I am the most loving, caring mother, wife, friend, and mentor that anyone could ever have.

It is fun to be known as witty, charming, warmhearted, non-judgmental, open for productive change, and an inspiring, powerful, professional woman who is courageously different in her own divine choice.

It is inspiring to be a graceful woman of prominence, who leads an extraordinary life and enriches others' lives in the process. I am self-reliant, highly optimistic, trustworthy, and I express myself freely.

I am enthusiastic...the power of light guides me, and I welcome new and exciting experiences, knowing that my inspiration, love, caring, and gratitude for life are making a difference in the world...and is the gift I return to the universe in recognition for the blessing of life.

I needed to heal; heal my spirit, my mind, and my soul. The only way to avoid patterns of negativity is to change the environment which has made you susceptible to making the wrong choices. As part of the healing process, I decided to wipe my personal slate clean and detox myself of all negativity, inside and out. I embarked upon a stringent, month-long fast that consisted of consuming only water and the purest of foods, and ridding myself of watching television or reading the newspaper, all so I could fill myself with positivity. I read books by some of the great thinkers of our time, and reached deep inside to *find* myself.

This journey has taken me on its share of twists and turns, bringing me to where I am now. Each day has brought growth, new attitudes, and new understandings of the world around me. As I have grown, my body has changed, and so, too, have my perceptions of people and their actions. Thought by thought, day by day, I have evolved into who and what I am today. I have made the conscious choice that when I look at the people around me, I can see the beauty in each one and appreciate the diversity that makes each person unique. We all have greatness within, even though we may become spiritually and emotionally lost, and appear to be wandering aimlessly through life. It is possible to find new direction by allowing the infinite spirit to show us the way. I have begun to practice this in my own life by releasing doubt and fear, and finding a way to let that infinite spirit flow through me in all its glory.

When we allow ourselves to be on the infinite path, we will always be on the right path or track. Every day I have discovered there is a reason for being where I am, and for learning the lessons in life that have been taught to me. This is an ongoing process which never stops, and is something we all possess. Faith sees 'all things,' while the mind does not.

> *If we live by the spirit, let us also be guided by the spirit.*
>
> —Galatians 5:25

For, I, the Lord your God, hold your right hand.
                                        — Isaiah 41:14

I was, and am, comforted by my consciousness/knowledge of the infinite spirit's presence, just as I am comforted and draw strength through the acknowledgement of my faith. My values support me, and causes me to be directed at all times. Each of us has the ability to do and become anyone we want to be. Birds do not fly because they have wings, but because they *want* to fly.

As I tried to repair my spirit from the ordeal that Nick and Tommy put me through, I had to remember that when I come to the edge of the light, and I am about to step into the darkness of the unknown, I can be assured of one thing: either the infinite spirit will provide solid ground for me to stand on, or I will be taught to fly.

One of the hardest tools to grasp is the principle of forgiveness. I can honestly say that I have been able to reach down deep within myself, and forgive Nick and Tommy for everything they did to me. I also had to forgive myself. Holding onto anger is like grasping a hot coal with the intent of throwing it at someone else; ultimately, it is you who will be burned. Forgiveness has been an important part of my process in growing stronger, moving forward, and seeking my divine purpose in life. Holding onto past regrets doesn't do anyone any good, as it resides in the past and is not worth resurrecting what is dead and buried. Marathons are run with one foot in front of the other—when you look backward, you stumble. For the sake of my children, I let go of all the resentment, hurt, and anger, releasing the past and leaving me free to move on to a productive future with a light heart and spirit. I gave my children the most humble and greatest of gifts…love. I live in the now, experience each moment as a good one, and know the future is joyous and secure for myself and my children. What I give out faithfully is being returned to me tenfold.

CHAPTER 10

Moving Forward

I may have been down, but I was not out; I would never be out. The only thing left for me to do was regroup and move forward from a position of knowledge and power. I would do whatever it took to have Hunter and Aidan back with me where they belonged. Justice is supposed to be fair; however, I have witnessed first-hand how the "attaboy" system works. It is not my intention to sound like a victim—far from it. I know my children will still love me. Sacrifice hurts and I continue to operate under the philosophy that there will come a day when it will all be worth it, and the odds will turn in your favor if you just believe.

I believe if it were up to my exes and their families, I would not continue to be a presence in my children's lives. I think it is their intention to wipe away the memories my children have of me, and relegate me to the status of second-class citizen where they are concerned.

This has been so apparent to me in my dealings with Tommy. While his collusion with Nick has been a fact of my life, it has been the presence of his new wife, Karen, that has caused me the greatest alarm with regard to Aidan's emotional and physical well-being. She has continually tried to insinuate herself into the role of mother to my child, while simultaneously attempting to edge me out of his life. She and Tommy have worked in concert to try to turn Aidan against me by waging a campaign of manipulation and treachery. While I have always bent over backward to accommodate the time Aidan spends with his father, the same courtesy has not been extended to me. I planned a welcome home party for Aidan one year after a lengthy separation, complete with balloons, streamers, signs, and snacks. I had invited all the neighborhood kids over—Aidan's playmates—for the party, and waited for Tommy to return him to me at the appointed time. My calls to Tommy and Karen went unanswered, and I resorted to texting them to provide documentation as to their violation of the custody agreement. I received an immediate call from Karen informing me Aidan was attending a birthday party, and they were running late. When they arrived with Aidan an hour and a half later, I asked my son if he'd had fun at the birthday party, to which he informed me he hadn't even been at a birthday party that day. Tommy's continual defiance of the court orders would force me to involve the authorities, which in essence would supply me with documented evidence for court. However, once again, none of this evidence was submitted to the court.

Perhaps the most cruel and hurtful action against me has been Tommy and Karen's efforts to brainwash Aidan since the trial. He's told me of times when I would come to pick him up and he could see me out the window, yet Karen and Tommy would tell him I would have to wait. He understands that his father is keeping us apart. There were times when we were together in the presence of his father and step-mother, and Aidan would refuse to have eye contact with me, or even hold my hand. When I finally asked him why he was acting that way, he informed me that Kay Kay, as he calls her, had told him not to talk to me or she would hurt him if he had any physical contact with me or showed me any affection whatsoever. In fact, he informed me, she had spanked him on multiple occasions when he'd invoked my name. I was incensed to learn this woman had carried out her threats of physical violence against my child, and that she was instructing him to deny me as his mother. I alerted Aidan's psychologist, who also expressed concern over Karen's actions toward my son, further stating she'd never heard him say anything positive where she was concerned, but had nothing but wonderful things to say about me. As a result of my trying to correct the damage Karen was inflicting upon Aidan, I was rewarded with a restraining order barring me from seeing my son for months. I was distraught beyond belief. I later received an additional restraining order after my mother was unable to accompany me on one of my trips, which triggered Tommy to prevent me from seeing Aidan for almost three months.

Aidan has also been forced to deny his brother, Hunter. He's been told that Hunter is not his brother, but that Karen's son, Cooper, is. Aidan has been threatened with yet more spankings if he mentions his brother's name. Hunter and Aidan are extremely close and love to play and laugh with each other every time they see each other. Whenever Hunter doesn't get to see his brother, he constantly asks me where he is and when can he see him again. Kaytlin has suffered as well by not being able to see her baby brothers, and has raged against Tommy for keeping Aidan from all of us. I have borne witness to the way my son cries until his little body shakes when Sundays come and it is time for me to pack his things and return him to Tommy and Karen. He would beg me to let him stay, telling me we hadn't had enough time with each other.

There were numerous other times where he would declare to me that he would not be returning to his father's house. When I would drop him off with Tommy, he would have to be forcibly peeled away from me, as he would plaster his little body against mine, refusing to let go, refusing to place his little feet upon the pavement. I would squeeze his hand and remind him to be strong, and that we wouldn't be apart forever. I would tell him this as much for him as for myself. There was another time when he asked if I had any pictures of him, as Karen had informed him I didn't carry any photographs of him at all. I pulled out all the photo albums I had of him from birth, documenting every aspect of his young life, and the smile that broke across his face upon seeing this both broke and buoyed my heart.

The worst atrocity was when Aidan tentatively asked me if I was his mom, as Karen had told him I was his step-mother and she was his mother, because she had been the one to carry him in her belly for nine months. Hearing my child utter these words was like someone had plunged a knife into my chest and dragged it across my insides. My mother overheard these horrible things, and assured Aidan that I was his mother and no one else.

I attempted to have primary custody of Aidan transferred back to me with visitation granted to Tommy, and to arrange for a midway drop-off/pickup point for Aidan's exchange. I have also tried to have the order that my mother accompany me on the trips to pick up Aidan modified, as she is frequently ill and unable to make these grueling drives with me every other weekend. Unfortunately, I have been unable to obtain a court date for visitation, and Tommy has not let me visit Aidan, but I won't give up. I can't. For me, to give up would send a signal to Aidan that his mother doesn't care, and I refuse to have him believe I would ever give up fighting to get him back.

Of course my dealings with Nick were no better. I continued to compile evidence of his abuse against me as well as his countless lies. I obtained the multiple 911 recordings of him coming to my home, threatening me and Kaytlin, and ripping Hunter from my arms. This was rock-solid proof, which should have resulted in him being arrested for assault and battery, not to mention the violation of an ex parte protective order I had managed to obtain (this order is equivalent to a protective order, good for a maximum of fourteen days). This order was violated on the day it was entered, and by rights Nick should have been thrown in jail immediately—no questions asked. After threatening Kaytlin and trespassing on my property multiple times (which was a violation of one of the few restraining orders I was able to get), Nick clearly should have been arrested. There was also an incident where I dropped off Hunter after my visitation and he began to yell at me, and hurl all sorts of nasty accusations at me. I pleaded with him to back off and leave in peace, but he continued his rampage, badmouthing Chad in front of his daughter, Piper. I spoke with an attorney in Austin, Texas, who informed me that the Montgomery County Police Department had foregone their duties with regard to these repeated violations, and indicated this neglect was a contributing factor in Nick not being correctly cited. Further, I discovered these multiple abuses perpetrated by Montgomery County law enforcement had been under investigation by the Texas Rangers years before, which has domain over cases of corruption in the state. I needed to find a judge who would listen to me; I needed to be able to present my case to a judge who would be fair and impartial.

By this point I didn't care if I was sent to jail for exposing the ruthless and corrupt acts I'd uncovered; the Supreme Court recently clarified that "our common law protects individuals from physical harm…that protection extends to the disclosure of information that substantially threatens such harm." It was incumbent upon me to tell the truth, and risk the consequences. If I was incarcerated, I would merely chalk it up as yet another ploy for the politically unethical in their attempts to shut me up and silence the voice of a law-abiding single mother. However, I was born a fighter and even in the face of so much injustice, I refused to give up on trying to get justice. It was shameful how money had been put ahead of the best interests of family.

No matter the uphill struggle I faced in trying to prove my case, I wouldn't give up.

I couldn't.

CHAPTER 11

Finding Inspiration

While Nick and Tommy lay at the root of many of my troubles, the corrupt judicial system of Montgomery County, Texas, played just as big a role in holding me down and legally stealing my children away from me. Both Nick and Tommy's families—especially my ex-husband's—held considerable sway over elected officials in Montgomery County, which was the impetus for entangling me in an endless cycle of court cases. Nick's family could be seen around town on numerous occasions having dinner with, attending fundraisers for, even going on hunting trips with these officials. In Texas judges are elected, and one of the judges who helped to facilitate injustice against me was one of the most corrupt, devious, and hypocritical judges in Montgomery County: Judge Tracy A. Gilbert. The more I learned about this elected official, who had been entrusted with doing right by the public, the more betrayed I felt and the more determined I was to shine a light on the unscrupulous practices of Montgomery County.

Some may think it foolish to take on a powerful person, much less an entire system. However, many revolutions can be traced to the courage and tenacity of those who were willing to stand up and demand a change to the status quo. Sometimes it can be a good thing to have enemies; it means you stood up for something. Were it not for groups and individuals who went before us, we might still have slavery, women might not be allowed to vote, factory workers might still work in deplorable conditions, and contaminated drinking water might still be coursing beneath the town of Hinkley, California (those of you who have seen the movie *Erin Brockovich* know what I am talking about). Cowering in fear or complacency never brings positive transformation; fear and complacency keep you stuck, keep you bound to a way of life that will only continue to plunge you into the depths of darkness and negativity.

What inspired me to begin pursuing this path toward toppling the corruption in Montgomery County was the case of Richard Fine. This one-time Beverly Hills attorney had uncovered massive government and judicial corruption that had been perpetrated against the taxpayers of his state; he was jailed and eventually disbarred for his actions on behalf of the citizens of California. Richard believes in order to get rid of corruption we must find competent candidates and then vote for them. His rallying cry began to ring in my head, as I realized the only way we can create change is through educating the public and electing ethical competent officials. One of the first things I knew had to change in my quest for justice would be the Texas judicial system, and it would have to be done from the inside.

Finding a qualified judicial candidate to run against Judge Gilbert would be important, but truthfully I wasn't actively seeking anyone to do so. However, I met Jessica Siegel through mutual friends, and as I learned more about her impressive background (a one-time associate with global law firm, Baker Botts, LLP, extensive experience in civil litigation, family law, wills and probate, not to mention a previous career as an engineer for NASA), I began to believe she might just be the person to help effect change within the Montgomery County Court system. I broached the subject with her, and while she expressed to me that she never thought of herself as someone who would seek political office, the more we discussed it, she, too, became more enthusiastic about the idea. I was so excited by the prospect, against my attorney's wishes, I offered to become Jessica's campaign manager. Frankly, by that point, what else did I have to lose?

As Jessica began to delve into research about the 418th District, and specifically about Judge Gilbert, we were shocked at what we uncovered.

Judge Gilbert presides over the 418th District Court, which was established by the Texas legislature to give preference to family law matters (it is the only court in Montgomery

County to do so). Judge Gilbert portrays himself as a family law specialist and dedicated family man who will throw the book at deadbeat dads. In truth, Judge Gilbert was later found to have fathered a son out of wedlock with a woman he engaged in a one-night stand. He never paid a dime in child support, and it would be seventeen years before he even acknowledged the child. It was only when the child's mother stepped forward to file suit for back child support that Judge Gilbert admitted the existence of his son. As the heat intensified over his personal life, the judge sought to have his paternity records sealed, claiming they had no bearing on his professional life. I couldn't disagree more; if your job is to preside over high-conflict custody cases, how you conduct your own custody issues is of paramount importance.

Judge Gilbert has also been shown to cross ethical lines in his cases, particularly by refusing to recuse himself in instances where there have been clear conflicts of interest. The list of cases where there have been clear canon violations in Judge Gilbert's courtroom is a long and ugly one.

One of the more disturbing cases we uncovered was that of Art Eden. This Wisconsin man was pulled into court by his ex-wife, a Montgomery County resident, when she sought to have Art stripped of his parental rights to their five-year-old daughter. The ex-wife prevailed, and Art's parental rights to his young daughter were terminated by Judge Gilbert. Termination of parental rights is usually seen as an extreme move, and one the courts avoid in favor of other alternatives, such as supervised visitation.

Eden did not receive a fair trial, because there was an ethical stain on the proceedings; Judge Gilbert's personal attorney, Steve Jackson, who was representing him in his own custody issues regarding his heretofore unknown teenage son, also served as counsel for Art's ex-wife. This fact was never disclosed in court, and Judge Gilbert did not recuse himself from the case. Art filed several motions to halt the trial, pointing out numerous concerns, including Judge Gilbert's blatant conflict; all of the motions were ignored by the judge. Eden's daughter was never appointed an amicus attorney (a neutral party meant to represent the best interest of the child, particularly in high-conflict custody cases). In Texas an amicus attorney is required by law "unless the court finds the interests of the child will be represented adequately by a party to the suit whose interests are not in conflict with the child's interests." Judge Gilbert declared no amicus was required, since Eden's ex-wife (and the child's mother) "had no interest adverse to the child." Considering this wasn't a case involving abuse of any kind on the part of the father toward the child, how could it be good for the daughter to be kept away from her other parent?

Eden was denied a pre-trial hearing and was unable to secure counsel due to his indigent status, which forced him to represent himself in court. He was held in contempt of court and sentenced to ninety days in jail—all because he dared to shine a light on Judge Gilbert's unethical practices.

Jackson told the *Houston Chronicle* that Judge Gilbert was "qualified" and a "fair jurist," and that his relationship with the judge, which dated back to elementary school, was a "disadvantage" in court because the court expected him to be "perfect." Houston family law attorney Brian J. Fischer, told the paper, "It would have been a slam-dunk motion to recuse." And yet, Judge Gilbert never did.

In my case Nick's attorney, Lynn Esposito, was seen with Judge Gilbert on several occasions discussing our custody case without the presence of my lawyer. This ex parte hearing, which a judge can decide to hold with the attendance of all parties involved, is widely considered to be improper. And yet it happened over and over again without my knowledge.

Stephanie was another litigant we uncovered who had passed through Judge Gilbert's courtroom, and suffered from the fraudulent practices perpetrated by him and Montgomery County. She filed for divorce from her husband, and later discovered that the attorney general's child support division had filed a petition on behalf of a former employer to establish paternity of her daughter and son. Stephanie wanted it made clear that because this was not an issue related to child support, there was no standing for the AG's office to become involved in the matter. Judge Gilbert allowed Cecelia Wilkenfeld, the representative from the AG's office, to intervene in Stephanie's divorce, attempting to have DNA testing performed on the children, even though the legally recognized parents did not wish this to be done (her soon to be ex-husband had claimed paternity for the children). A gag order was even issued against the children to prevent an investigation against the former employer regarding allegations of physical and sexual abuse. Even though reports from the sheriff's department, Child Protective Services, and Children's Safe Harbor (an advocacy organization) all found strong evidence the children had been abused, this proof was disallowed.

Eventually, Stephanie maintains, she met with Wilkenfeld, who informed her that the paternity motion being dropped; however, she was later informed a child support case had been opened in her name. In attempting to get records regarding this alleged case, they were found to be non-existent. She was served a motion by the amicus attorney requesting additional funds for services, even though, once again, no records were on file. She was told the matter would be discussed during trial. When Stephanie appeared in court and asked why she was being tried, she was informed it was for her divorce, which by then had been nonsuited, a fact she had to remind Judge Gilbert about. Further, Wilkenfeld denied ever meeting with Stephanie, and that the paternity matter was still active. Despite having evidence to the contrary, she maintains Judge Gilbert denied her the opportunity to present her case. As she did not live in the jurisdiction area, she tried several times to have her case transferred out of the 418th District Court of Montgomery County, only to be given the runaround by Judge Gilbert's clerk.

The nightmare continued for Stephanie as she was arrested for taking her children out of state on a vacation, though she maintains she informed the judge of her intention to do so. Unfortunately she served three months in jail, costing her precious time with her children, a criminal charge, and the ability to fight her case.

Subsequently, all of Stephanie's motions were denied, and numerous judgments were entered against her and her ex-husband into the court records. The parental rights of the children's legal father was terminated, and custody of the children in question were awarded to the ex-employer, who eventually admitted in court filings he wasn't the children's biological father and was alleged to have physically and sexually abused the children. Worse, she found her case information had been altered, including the certified copies of her trial transcripts, which showed her making alleged admissions during prior hearings. The ex-employer was overheard telling people that Stephanie's first ex-husband had used his influence as a federal investigator to influence the outcome of her case. A follow-up e-mail confirmed this to be the case, and Stephanie is certain his actions are in retaliation for having his parental rights to their now-teenage son terminated in 1998. Stephanie has stated she is unable to seek proper legal recourse and is terrified of Judge Gilbert's influence.

This only scratches the surface of what I have uncovered about Montgomery County's unethical practices, including the sanctioning of illegal arrests, presiding over cases where there is no jurisdiction, and obstructing justice. There were repeated incidents of Judge Gilbert's personal attorney's utilizing the same forensic psychologists, who in turn would recommend supervised visitation with the non-custodial parent, even though there was never any evidence to support a need to do so. We even learned of one case where a woman lost full custody to her ex, even though he was in a wheelchair, paralyzed from the neck down. The father was unable to care for himself, yet was entrusted with the care of young children. One case concerned a seventeen-year marriage where the wife had always been a stay-at-home mom and lost custody of both children and her home, and received no community property from her ex-husband, a doctor. Judge Gilbert told her to get a job and pay child support, and that the abuse she suffered during the divorce proceedings was to be expected. He further told her that in any case there is one party who wins and one who loses, and there is nothing anyone can do to change his orders.

There were several instances where Judge Gilbert's personal attorneys would represent litigants in cases he was presiding over. The relationships were never disclosed in court, and he never recused himself. Worse, these attorneys won their cases each and every time. Judge Gilbert was also found to show favor to particular law firms in exchange for campaign donations—in other words, awarding custody of children to the highest bidder. Even after I personally spent $186,000, it wasn't enough for me to retain custody of my children in Judge Gilbert's courtroom, or receive my frequently requested protective orders.

It was heartbreaking and yet motivating to learn about

the corruption. Now that we were working from a point of knowledge, it would empower us to move ahead with our plans to effect true and positive change within the system.

The day arrived for Jessica to declare her candidacy, and as her campaign manager I would accompany her to the Montgomery County Republican Party Headquarters in Conroe to make it official. We left her house full of excitement and happiness about what lay ahead in the future.

We had no idea what was waiting for us.

CHAPTER 12

Fight for Justice

Supporting Jessica any way I could in this endeavor was as important to me as it was to her. We knew we had an uphill battle, but we believed in the power of the system, and more importantly we believed in our power to *change* the system. It wouldn't be easy, and it would take a lot of courage on both our parts. We couldn't imagine just how much of our mettle would be tested.

The day Jessica and I were to file her paperwork, I received a phone call from a friend, Trisha Shafer, who'd had her own ongoing issues with Montgomery County and Judge Gilbert specifically. Trish had been embroiled in her own troubles with the Montgomery County legal system. Her first encounter revolved around her attempts to try to unravel the mysterious death of her uncle while he was incarcerated in the Montgomery County jail. The autopsy photos show evidence of a severe beating while behind bars, including cuts, severe bruising all over his body, crushed kneecaps, a fist-sized depression and skull fracture, and a gunshot wound. Yet his death was ruled to be from natural causes due to heart disease.

While trying to settle her multimillion-dollar lawsuit against Montgomery County for her uncle's death, which was dropped, unbeknownst to her at the time, by her own attorney, Trish was simultaneously battling her ex in Judge Gilbert's court for custody of her kids. Trish's case is a prime example of how incidents can be twisted against you and can bring you to your knees.

Trish sent her father-in-law a series of text messages where she relayed that she had asked her emotionally abusive husband to leave their home, saying she had kicked him out. Already in the midst of a bitter custody dispute, Trish was slapped with a protective order by her ex under the advice of his attorney, Grady James, who offered up altered versions of the text messages (that she "kicked him," eliminating the crucial "out" part of the text) as proof of her "abusive behavior." (When a person is shown to have perpetrated family violence, that person has no claim to custody under Family Code.) She hired a new attorney to defend her in court and present the full versions of the text messages. She was dismayed when her attorney presented only a few pages of her text messages. This maneuver on the part of her husband and his legal team (which included Mr. James, whose daughter was the associate judge in Judge Gilbert's courtroom) allowed him to get a protective order and limit access to her children.

Her husband, with the help of Grady James, continued to work the system and defy previously agreed upon orders, such as visitation with her children and pulling them out of school, though he was not allowed to do so. After a scheduled visit with her children, Trish dropped them off at his home for Father's Day weekend and was stunned to find another restraining order had been issued against her, keeping her from her children for two weeks.

After many more legal tactics by Mr. James, including non-suiting the custody case that was being heard by another judge within the county, which Trish was winning, she found herself placed in front of Judge Gilbert (with the attorney who had just dropped her lawsuit spectating in the courtroom), and she lost custody to her ex. She further learned her ex-husband had concealed the existence of a trust fund from her (half of which she was entitled to), leaving her with nothing. After the custody trial and the re-opening of her uncle's wrongful death lawsuit, Trish became a target of Montgomery County. While out driving, she was stopped for failure to signal, for going a few miles over the speed limit, subjected to random "well-checks" during the day, and slapped with a DWI charge. To fight these ridiculous charges, she retained criminal attorneys who never let her see the evidence on which she was charged. She started getting harassing calls and text messages. An attorney from the county was even so bold as to send a photograph of his penis in exchange for legal advice. Unbeknownst to her, her driver's license was suspended, which meant she was driving on a suspended license. She was no longer able to work, which triggered a judgment against her for failing to meet her child support obligations. She was required to wear an alcohol monitor around her ankle, have a breathalyzer in her car, and submit to random urinary analysis—and she had to pay for all of these indignities before even going to trial.

Trish alerted me to her intention to file a formal judicial complaint against Judge Gilbert for disallowing evidence in her case and a state bar complaint against J.D. Lambright for attorney misconduct in handling the lawsuit with her uncle. Knowing what she would be up against, I agreed to accompany her to the courthouse for moral support. The judicial system is frightening and overwhelming, and many people are scared when they must face any type of legal proceeding, no matter how small or inconsequential it may seem. My research has shown that the more moral support you receive in instances like this, the more likely you are to stand your ground with regard to your legal fight. Knowing this, I was happy to give Trish the help.

As Trish filed her complaint with the district clerk's office, she was summoned to Judge Gilbert's chambers under the guise of receiving assistance from the judge on her custody case. It was suspicious, as Trish had been asking for help with her case for up to two years and had received nothing. I stayed by her side as we went to the courtroom of the 418th District, and as we approached I was filled with a sense of dread, a silent but steady pounding in my heart that something wasn't right with the situation. The whispers were deafening. Trish was pulled into the judge's juror chamber (I wasn't allowed in), and the next thing I knew, a teary Trish was being arrested on a revocation warrant from her DWI in a family courtroom. I was in utter shock as she handed me all of her paperwork, begging me to get the word out to her family about what was going on. I tried to calm her down, and promised we would all work to get her released as soon as possible, as the bailiff, Officer Shanahan, shut the door in my face.

As I made my way to Jessica's house, I contacted Trish's family members so they could begin the process of obtaining her release. I knew the charges against Trish were trumped up, and direct retaliation for her daring to stand up against the unethical practices of Judge Gilbert and Montgomery County. What I had witnessed made me that much stronger in my resolve that I was doing the right thing by working with Jessica to go within the system to spur change.

To avoid any complications, I advised Jessica that we should wait until the last possible moment to file her paperwork. We were a little nervous, but enthusiastic about her candidacy. This was the right thing to do for all the right reasons.

As Jessica, her seven-year-old son, and I made our way to Conroe, two separate cars swerved at us. Initially, we brushed it off, chalking it up to distracted, impatient drivers on a Friday afternoon. However, as we drew closer to the courthouse, one of the cars, which was black with government plates, went directly at us, trying—it seemed—to hit us and possibly force us off the road. As I've been followed around Montgomery County many times by various private investigators and local law enforcement agencies, I knew my car was familiar, and it occurred to me that someone was after us. I would not be deterred, however, and we proceeded to the Republican headquarters.

We were greeted by Dr. Walter Wilkerson, Chairman of the Montgomery County Republican Party, and he couldn't have been more gracious or helpful in walking us through the filing process. The excitement of the moment was palpable; we were full of smiles and anticipation. It's not every day someone takes the step of running for public office. We'd brought Jessica's seven-year-old son with us so he could witness this monumental moment in his mother's life, and snapped a ton of pictures as Jessica officially filed her candidacy paperwork.

Within moments, a DA official, followed by a Texas Ranger, strode in. Dr. Wilkerson asked if we knew who these people were, and of course we didn't. The Texas Ranger informed Jessica she was being arrested for submitting fraudulent information on a notarized document, and slapped handcuffs on her over her protests that she'd done nothing wrong. She was informed that her arrest had to do with not meeting the residency requirements to run for public office, and that Jessica would need to take up the matter with the judge at her arraignment. Her young son watched as his mother was led away in handcuffs. I was stunned at what happened, and my heart went out to Jessica's little boy for having to witness such a traumatic scene.

I was more than a little convinced that the long arm of corruption in Montgomery County had reached out yet again to slap us.

Judicial candidates are required to live in their county where they are filing for a period of twenty-four consecutive months. Jessica had moved to the area in late 2010, and had previously filed to run for the seat. During the time of her original application, she inadvertently omitted months of her residency, so her application was denied. However, due to redistricting in Texas there was a second filing period, and she was advised she could refile. It was at that time law enforcement officials rushed in to arrest her, claiming she had once again submitted false information. We all knew that just like the situation with Trish, this was a bogus charge and knew we would prevail; we had the truth on our side.

The next few hours were a blur, as I put out calls, texts, and e-mails to everyone I knew, alerting them to the situation. I was contacted by the *Conroe Courier*, the weekly community paper, to update them on Jessica's situation. The paper had already been aware of Jessica's intent to file, and were tipped off about this latest turn of events. The *Courier's* story hit the Web, and their coverage of the story spurred phone calls from the *Houston Chronicle*, the Texas Bureau of the Associated Press, the ABC station in Houston, and many more media outlets. Since I was with Jessica when she was arrested, reporters were interested in the inside perspective I could provide, and I gave media interviews well into the early morning hours. I expressed how mortified I was that a judge who runs on a platform of being an advocate for families has a woman arrested in front of her young son—what kind of message does that send to the community? This is supposed to be a democratic society where everyone who meets the requirements should be allowed to run for public office and we let the voters decide. Jessica's arrest demonstrated that in Montgomery County, if you run against the wrong person, you could get arrested.

Jessica was forced to spend the night in jail on a $21,500 bond. She was released on Saturday afternoon after her bond was lowered to $3,000, and by then I had formulated a plan. It was clear to us that Jessica's arrest was an attempt to silence us about what we knew with regard to Montgomery County's unethical courtroom practices. I'd been a longtime victim of the court system in the county, and the media interest in Jessica's case provided us with the perfect platform to get our story out into the public. The next step was logical.

We needed to go national.

CHAPTER 13

The Nation's Capital

Overnight, Jessica's arrest became the number one story on the Associated Press wire, and when news of Judge Gilbert's custody case hit the press, the blogosphere exploded. The public and the media began to demand accountability from the judge, and encouraged voters to look more closely at the man who'd painted himself as a beacon of family morality and justice.

We knew we needed to take this story national, and the best place to do that was Washington, DC.

I had been thinking about going to DC for quite some time. While one voice can be strong, collective voices produce a roar. During the past year, I had utilized Facebook to get my story out to the public, and in doing so I touched a nerve. I began to hear from people across the country who had also been victimized by a corrupt and callous court system. I also became an active participant in several forums on corruption and advocacy. It was through my participation in these various, social networking environments that I was contacted by a local watchdog news blog for an in-depth report on my story. I was elated; this bit of exposure could be exactly what I needed to generate some forward movement on my cases. In the wake of the article being published, the publisher, Joey, was arrested by a Texas Ranger and thrown in jail for ninety days. He and I both knew who was responsible. I did continue to reach out to other media outlets, but was met with resistance; some media shared with me they were reticent to take on these powerful and politically connected families, afraid of losing their jobs. I can't say I was surprised, considering how many people in my life have lost their livelihoods due to unethical practices; others were disinterested, since I was only one voice. In order to be heard I needed more voices, yet as many people as I heard from, several were reluctant to speak up. I had to keep pressing on though.

The situation with Jessica presented a phenomenal opportunity to bring national attention to the problem. Never in a million years did any of us think a judicial candidate would be arrested, and in the end it provided a catalyst for us to take action. It was important we talk to as many people we could, from lawmakers to lobbyists, to community activists to major media. People had been trying to silence us through intimidation, and we weren't going to take it anymore. It was time to rip open this ugly wound and expose it in all of its nastiness. Once the sun shines on the dirt, there's no more hiding it.

Once we'd made the decision, there was no stopping us. The whispers were loud and clear. I met Jessica when she was released from jail, and was horrified to see a large and ugly bruise across her cheek. I worried she'd been physically abused while behind bars, but she assured me the bruise occurred when she fell off the wire bench she'd been forced to sleep on during the night. I was outraged; this was a woman who had dedicated her life to helping people through the use of the legal system, and now that entire legal community had turned its back on her and put her in jail as a criminal. I just couldn't see the justice.

Admittedly, we didn't have a firm plan about what we would do when we got to the nation's capital. Jessica had family in the area, and we would rely on them to help us crystallize the details of what we would need when we arrived to help us get our message out. After the events of Friday, we thought it would be best to get out of town quickly. We couldn't be sure if any retaliatory measures would be exacted against us, and therefore thought it best to hit the road. In fact I forfeited my weekend with Hunter, as I couldn't be sure if anyone would come after me while he was in my care. If sacrificing a bit of time with my son one weekend meant I could get him back for good, the forfeiture was worth it.

Jessica, her son, and I took off Saturday evening and drove straight through to the Carolinas before finally stopping at a hotel for some much needed rest and regrouping. Finally Trish, who fortunately had been released from jail, was flown to DC later in the week, and we rolled into Washington, DC ready to pound the pavement.

CHAPTER 14

Washington, DC

We knew we'd be in DC the week that Congress would be in session, which provided a prime opportunity for us. Jessica's brother and sister-in-law are also attorneys, and being Jewish have significant ties to the community from both legal and religious standpoints. As a group we sat down and hammered out a strategy for making contact with all the key lawmakers on both a state and a national level. The family also advised us to reach out to the FBI and the US Attorney's office, which is charged with the investigation of corruption in our court system. We were also put in touch with representatives of the secret service, who counseled us on what agencies we would need to visit, and the best people for us to take our story to once we got there.

During our strategy session, we met Art, an alumnus of

Georgetown University. Upon hearing our story, which was so similar to his own, he vowed to help us in any way he could. True to his word, he and I took a trip to the Library of Congress. Except for a few librarians, the building was empty and we breezed right in with no problems. While there we tracked down phone numbers—including the personal cell phone numbers—of our nation's lawmakers. We pored over phone books, gathering the numbers for these agencies, and making appointments to come by and share our story with them. We had reams of pages filled with the contact information for some of the most powerful people in Washington, DC. I didn't find out until later the Library of Congress is restricted, and requires special access badges for entry!

We worked round-the-clock burning up the phone lines to make appointments with as many people as we could. When assistants would put us off, we'd utilize cell phone numbers and reach out to lawmakers directly. It was exhausting, though in many ways it felt as though we were lobbyists, and in a way we were—we were lobbying for the children.

After we'd been in town for a few days preparing our research and strategy, we were ready. Early in the morning, we hit the steps of Congress armed with fliers we'd created that told the story of Jessica's arrest, along with the damning information we'd uncovered about the corruption in Montgomery County and our own personal stories of persecution and horror at the hands of so many unethical people. It was an incredible relief to be able to speak openly and freely. We had been gagged for so long, and we hadn't even known it. Through the course of the morning, we stopped hundreds of senators, representatives, congressmen, and congresswomen, gave them our information, and told them a little bit about our story, stressing that if we had to go into the witness protection program to ensure the truth was told, we were willing to do so. Many of the people we spoke with sympathized with us and urged us to keep spreading the word about what we had uncovered.

After an exhilarating morning coming into contact with so many powerful people, it was time for us to make the rounds of various politicians we specifically wanted to make contact with. We knew we wanted to get in front of Senator Kay Bailey Hutchison, who at the time represented Texas; US Representative Shelia Jackson Lee, known for being extremely outspoken in her beliefs; and Representative John Conyers, a passionate advocate for civil liberties. We were elated to have the opportunity to visit their offices and sit down with them to tell our stories. They each took the time to listen to what we had to say as well as give us additional guidance about who we should speak to. We continued with our vigorous follow-up, coming in contact with even more individuals who could help strengthen our cause.

One of the most influential and comforting people Trisha and I had the honor of meeting was Rabbi Harold White, a nationally renowned spiritual advisor and community leader. Rabbi White was appointed as Jewish Chaplin of Georgetown University, making him the first rabbi to be appointed to a ministry position at a Catholic university. We met Rabbi White through Art's connections and were invited into his home for spiritual counsel. When we arrived he could sense our nervousness, and perhaps the high level of emotion we were all experiencing that day. He encouraged us to calm down, and think centered, tranquil thoughts, and even invited us to join him at his table for evening prayers. Though I am not Jewish, I was humbled to be included in this sacred ritual. Rabbi White spoke with us at length, listening with great interest and empathy as we told him how necessary it had been for us to flee from Texas, and how we'd come to DC seeking justice for ourselves and others. During our time with the rabbi, we met his personal assistant, who shared his own story of how he'd fallen in with the wrong people, and in turn had committed terrible crimes; he was sentenced to life in prison. However, through much personal work and turning himself over to his faith and the rabbi, he was able to see potential for his future and, in fact, Rabbi White was able to secure a pardon for him. If I didn't believe in the power of miracles before that meeting, I certainly did after hearing this man's inspirational story.

Rabbi White informed us that because of Jessica's heritage, she was under the Jewish "umbrella," and assured us that should anything happen to us he would take care of it. He encouraged us to keep going, and to follow up with the people we'd come in contact with, because that was key. He also took our fliers and promised to get the information into the hands of top-notch leaders and spread the word for us.

The compassion and caring this man showed to us reduced me to tears. I was so overcome with emotion that all I could do was throw my arms around him and sob my ongoing desire for a normal life for me and my children.

It was an amazing experience.

Exhausted but exhilarated, Trish and I continued to pound the pavement the following day, as Jessica had to fly back to Texas. We still hadn't had an opportunity to reach out to any DC media, among the most powerful in the nation, and to be honest, we weren't quite sure where to start. I hit upon the idea of asking our cab driver who the top media in town were, and specifically what the number one radio station in DC was. He immediately pointed us toward news personality Ernie Brown, a veteran broadcaster dedicated to exposing injustices. He offered to take us to the station, and advised us to start small, then go big with our story.

Although the executive offices of the station were closed for the evening, as luck would have it there was a gentleman getting off the elevator. Our T-shirts ("I'm the One Who Got Away") caught his eye, and we seized the opportunity to tell him why we were in town. He was so enthralled by what we had to say, he immediately told us he would introduce us to the owner of the station, who just happened to still be there. We were able to spend some time with the station owner and handed him our evidence. It turns out he had been keeping a close eye on the Texas prison system, which was being privatized into order to keep jails at ninety-eight percent capacity, so what we had to say was of great interest to him. The station owner suggested we speak with US Marshalls, and even put us in touch with some on the phone as we sat in his office. We were able to get on the radio that night and be interviewed, all while sending our information to other media in town using that station's fax machine! With the help of those contacts, we were able to secure three additional television interviews while we were in DC.

Almost from the moment we got to town, we were told that we would need to meet with the judicial committee, as that is the office charged with investigating judicial violations, the FBI for public corruption, and the US attorney. We were thrilled when we were able to land a meeting with a Texas state judicial board official. To our surprise and, I must say, elation, we discovered they were quite familiar with Montgomery County—in fact, they already had an investigation underway. Of course, they couldn't comment on any ongoing investigations, but did ask that we leave all of our evidence with them and pass along anything else we uncovered. The implications of being under this federal probe were huge; any case he'd had in his court was there, and if he were found to have even a hint of impropriety, his rulings could potentially be overturned. It meant I could finally get my protective orders. It meant the person who had physically and emotionally abused me in front of my children would be punished to the fullest extent of the law. It meant I would get justice. It meant I would get my kids back.

We stayed in DC for two weeks, knocking on doors, shaking hands, and making connections. We were introduced to an independent filmmaker who expressed interest in making a movie out of our story. I believe in addition to the compelling elements of our tale, what really attracted the interest was just being ourselves. The producer even referred to me as being the next Erin Brockovich, and told me I resembled Julia Roberts. I'm not looking for fame and glory; I just want to get my kids back. We sent him a synopsis of our story, so we'll see if anything comes from the meeting. We toured the campus of Georgetown University, and visited every major monument in the city, soaking in the history and feeling secure in our decision to go there.

I consider Washington, DC to be the trip of a lifetime.

CHAPTER 15

Children's Justice Foundation

During our time on the steps of Congress, and in our subsequent meetings, the germ of an idea began to take root. While most people took our fliers, we were repeatedly asked if we were part of an official organization or nonprofit, promising they would help us with any foundation we had. Shelia Jackson Lee in particular asked if we had a website that housed all of our information. In this day and age, being able to click onto a website during down time and gather information is increasingly where our world is headed. As I thought about all the drama I'd been subjected to with Nick and Tommy, and how the victims in those battles were Hunter and Aidan, it began to dawn on me that I could use these experiences and put them to great use.

A lightbulb went off.

While the resounding theme was to get a website, I actually had a much bigger vision. For quite some time, I'd had an idea about developing classes for judges that would teach them techniques to limit the emotional trauma children go through during high-conflict custody cases. I wanted to give parents involved in bitter custody battles the tools for successful co-parenting, and strategies they could employ to get along in a peaceful manner for the welfare of the child. I wanted to help people navigate through a complex and frightening system in order to mitigate them feeling as though they were being bullied or taken advantage. In keeping with my newfound outlook on life, I wanted to turn my negative experiences around into a positive.

As a result the Children's Justice Foundation was born.

I had studied psychology quite extensively as my major in school, so I was already in touch with many professors as a result. I had attended law school, and certainly my experience in and out of courtrooms had given me much familiarity with the legal system. I felt confident that I was the right person to lead this charge.

My vision for the foundation was to tap into local churches, particularly the larger ones, and utilize their space to teach four- to six-hour co-parenting classes. As part of the class, I wanted to make an updated video about custody cases and co-parenting. I had seen the ones produced by Montgomery County, and found them to be outdated and irrelevant. There is extensive, updated research about the emotional impact bitter divorces can have on children, the resulting custody cases, and separating siblings. My idea was to cater primarily to parents, and to give professionals the opportunity to use the classes for continuing education credits. I wanted to teach the legal community, including judges, attorneys, and mediators, how to minimize the emotional impact on children, and how their decisions can impact children as adults. I wanted to teach everyone the importance of communication, and how that vital skill can mean so much to the co-parenting structure. If a two-parent home isn't feasible, co-parenting is the absolute best way to shepherd a child through their adolescence. Prolonged custody battles only tear the children apart. Some attorneys believe it's best to keep children out of adult business; however, kids are smart. They have brains just like we do, and they pay attention to what goes on around them, even when we think they're not listening. I wanted to branch out and evolve into a major non-profit, such as a Big Brother, Big Sister type of organization, and provide mentorship to people who came through our doors. Providing tailored attention to kids was also key. Some children might benefit better around other children, so I decided to create get-together nights that would include games and food, so that the kids could spend time together in a fun, stress-free, and safe environment.

One of the most vital elements of the foundation would be the access to counselors for one-on-one sessions. I had my children participate in counseling sessions in order to ease their anxiety and give them a safe haven from the chaos swirling around them, and it made a tremendous difference in their demeanor and overall peace of mind. Currently, the way the legal system works is a child will meet with a court-appointed psychiatrist, who will ask endless probing—and sometimes leading—questions about each parent. Children can sometimes feel threatened in this environment and be afraid to reveal how they really feel about a situation. With the organization, I wanted to set it up so children would have mentors; any resultant issues during the one-on-one sessions would be addressed with both parents, and a plan of action would be decided upon by all parties. This would remove stressors from the child and prevent judicial decisions being based on one-time evaluations or hurried observations.

With my experience in DC, coupled with the visualization I had for my foundation and the emotional wringer I'd been through with Nick and Tommy, I began to formulate what the real definition of justice is and what it stands for. The power some individuals wield goes above and beyond where justice supposedly lies. Justice is supposed to be blind. However, in some cases, justice can be sold to the highest bidder. I have to ask, at what cost? My children were sold to the highest bidder. All of my children will feel the wrath of the choices made by others; it will manifest within them for years, well into adulthood. It will impact their relationships with friends, family, even romantic partners. I knew there were others out there just like me who, along with their children, were dealing with the long-term effects of their custody disputes. I was being presented with a unique opportunity to be a vessel of evolution and hope. The path I needed to tread was clear.

There were many people in my life who were fearful, even angry with me for going to Washington DC to stand up and shout. I saw it as a highly strategic move on my part. I went up against the system that tried to gag me, Trish, and Jessica. I wouldn't back down; I am standing strong. I've been told by so many people to just give up, to admit defeat. I will never do that. My children know I love them, and they love me—nothing would break that bond. They know I'm the best mom they could have ever had. If I have to sacrifice a few years with them, then that is what I will do. There are hundreds of families passing through family court in Montgomery County. By speaking up I can impact not just my life but so many people's lives; what I've done is for the betterment of everybody. I have my head on straight, and my shoulders are pushed back with pride. I accomplished what I set out to do.

One of my former attorneys reached out to me when I got home, and point blank said, "Jennie, you fucked up. You have no idea what you've done. You could lose custody."

All I could do was smile and ask, "Don't you see the beauty of what I did?" My judge wouldn't recuse himself, people were trying to gag us, we have been bullied by the court system, and I finally aimed the spotlight square on the people and on a system that prided itself on the perpetration of corruption. By the thoughtful look on his face, I could see he began to realize there was truth in what I was saying. He smiled and said, "Evidently, you *have* thought about this."

I threw myself into developing the Children's Justice Foundation, establishing a Facebook page, filing the proper paperwork to incorporate my nonprofit, and organizing local fundraisers. As soon as the Facebook page went up, counselors, parents, and retired judges started coming out of the woodwork, flooding me with their stories, and offers to help get government funding and sponsorship, as well as participate. There aren't many organizations out there providing the resources of the Children's Justice Foundation; clearly I'd struck a chord.

My story is not just about me, but everyone out there who has been victimized by a system that was supposed to protect them. I don't want anyone else to go through the horrors I've gone through. I can save other people. This is bigger than me. I can't ask, "Why me?" and think it's because I've been the continual recipient of bad luck. I can ask, "Why me?" and wonder what path God has chosen for me in this life. There have been many times when I've asked myself why all of these horrible things have happened to me. Sometimes, God makes things happen so you can get on the path you're supposed to be on. I have always known there was something bigger and greater, something with a deeper purpose, that I was supposed to be doing. I never knew what it was.

Knowing that I was a great mother, an outstanding employee, and a good person with a good heart, I just couldn't fathom why so many bad things kept happening. I know now. I've finally found my way.

CHAPTER 16

Continuing the Fight

As I worked to establish my foundation, I, of course, kept up the fight for my children. I found a new attorney, and we began the process of poring through the ten boxes of evidence I had pertaining to my custody cases, and all the mistakes and violations that occurred, including the numerous modification orders between the judges in my cases with Nick and Tommy, the ex parte meetings, altered evidence, and multiple other illegal actions were uncovered. It was gratifying to know that I finally had someone working on my side for a change.

Unfortunately, I continued to be kept from Aidan, as Tommy and Nick persisted in filing numerous modification orders against me. One of the conditions of my picking up my son for visitation was that my mother accompany me on the drive from Dallas to Houston. However, as Tommy knew, my mother became ill and was no longer able to make that eight-hour round-trip drive. He used that fact to keep my son away from me. I continued to be concerned about the impact on Aidan by his going for months without seeing his mom, and the influence Tommy's wife would have on him. I worried about the psychological impact, and even the possible physical consequences he might suffer as a result of being away from me. I continued to file motions to modify our custody arrangement and get Aidan back under my primary care. He was so unhappy living with his father and stepmother, and it made my heart ache that we were missing so much time together, that he was being forced to deny his brother, Hunter, and that he might be suffering irreparable harm being under their roof.

We went to court for the motion to vacate on the basis of the recusal evidence where I filed to have Aidan returned to me. I was concerned when an administrative judge, Judge Underwood, decided to sit on the bench during my hearing. He knew who I was, and my intuition told me something was awry. My gut feeling was correct, as the judge threw it out, calling it a "frivolous lawsuit." Unfortunately, and I'm not sure why, my attorney didn't say anything in court about me obtaining visitation with Aidan. I was never called to the stand to testify, and worse, I was ordered to pay legal fees amounting to $3,000 to Tommy's attorney. It was such a discouraging experience, though the one bright spot was that the mental evaluation ordered by the court deemed that supervised visits were unnecessary. However, I was dismayed to learn Tommy was allowed on two separate occasions to be interviewed by Dr. Joan Anderson, who was handling my evaluation, which I felt had to be a violation of the Health Insurance Portability and Accountability Act (HIPAA), and shown private investigator reports that demonstrated that the stalking continued. And yet, I was still denied protection from this criminal behavior.

Eventually, I reached the point where I was unable to pay my attorney. Though he had tried to help, he continued to run up against brick walls. Requests for communication from Nick and Tommy's attorneys continued to be ignored, and he even faced issues obtaining transcripts from court reporters. Even as an attorney, he could not get court clerks to set a court date that would grant me some type of visitation with Aidan. Faced with not being able to afford his services, I ultimately made the decision to go in pro se, or acting as my own attorney. No one would fight harder for my kids than I would, and no one knew more about my cases than I did.

Nick continued to play deadly games with me where Hunter was concerned. As my profile increased in the community with the establishment of my foundation, and the buzz about my story began to grow, he unbelievably stepped up his campaign toward me. He expressed he was concerned that my crusade could result in Hunter being "caught in the crossfire," and as a result filed a motion to have my visitation with Hunter reduced from standard to four hours twice a month, signed by Judge Gilbert. In addition my friendship with Trish drew his ire, and he slapped yet another order against me stating she could not be around Hunter. Nick also continued to drain my finances. Although I was already paying him $700 a month in child support plus insurance, he repeatedly sent me health insurance claims; one was for $900 in one month. I simply didn't have it. I was already living at home with my parents, my savings were gone, my 401(k) was empty, and I had no job prospects in sight. My attempts to have the child support order lowered were denied. Nick threatened to take me back to court for contempt. I filed a motion to have Judge Gilbert recuse himself from my case to avoid any impropriety due to my association with Jessica. He declined the order, which was cosigned by the administrative judge, confirming the non-recusal. I knew right then and there I would never receive a fair trial in Montgomery County. The cover-up was continuing.

I felt like giving up. I felt like closing the door on the world and staying inside, because it seemed as though every time there was a glimmer of hope, it would be snuffed out and I would be plunged into darkness once more. However, whenever I began to feel as though I just couldn't go on, I would remember that first and foremost I was Hunter and Aidan's mom, and I would push through those feelings of despair and pick myself up for them. They meant the world to me, and I never wanted them to think I gave up on trying to reunite our family.

CHAPTER 17

The Next Chapter

L ife took another series of dramatic turns. While some were negative, many others were positive, and ones that I believed would set my personal life on the right path for the first time in years, and most importantly, where Aidan and Hunter were concerned.

Jessica's name was put back on the ballot for the judicial race we'd fought so hard for her to be a part of, affording us a major triumph. Unfortunately, it did not result in the outcome we'd hoped for; Jessica lost the race and Judge Gilbert was allowed to retain his seat in the 418th Judicial District in Montgomery. While it was a stunning blow, I took some comfort that in spite of Jessica coming to the race late and being relatively unknown to voters in Montgomery County, she still took twenty-five percent of the vote. I attributed this to the notoriety her arrest generated, along with our subsequent efforts in DC. While it was disheartening that she lost, I still counted her candidacy as a victory. Many in Montgomery County had tried to prevent us from spilling their dirty little secrets. By being able to tell our story to so many people during our time in DC, we'd still managed to open up some eyes and gain some real traction for our cause. Sadly, Jessica has struggled to secure regular employment, and has been forced to move in with her daughter while she tries to get back on her feet. I believe her inability to move back into the legal sector is a result of her involvement of uncovering the corruption within Montgomery County.

Trish was arrested after the election for a protective order violation, of which there was none. She was able to present rock-solid proof that she'd never abused her husband, and therefore she didn't lose visitation with her children against Grady James in the courtroom. She was able to prove that the handling of her uncle's case was dealt with unethically, and the county attorney is now under investigation from the state bar. She'll get a new trial, and a new opportunity to get her kids back. I was so thrilled for her—she's trumped them!

We both have endured retaliation from Montgomery County since the election with what seemed to be endless court battles and restraining orders to keep us from our children; however, we get stronger with each battle, and we did achieve being filmed for the upcoming movie *Lawless*

America. I have been approached to begin a second book that will be very detailed about the evidence and corruption within the county—that's currently underway. Trish tells me to keep my head up, and I am, higher than ever.

Chad, of course, was someone else in my life who'd been forced to endure indignities and humiliation at the hands of my ex and his machinations. While the outside pressures we were under had been too much for us to bear, we continued to keep tabs on each other's lives. He fought back against the arrest warrant that had landed him in jail in Texas, as well as defend himself against the charges his ex's father had leveled against him, and assorted other charges trumped up by Nick. In the end, he was vindicated, all charges against him were dropped, and he even won his civil case. Lynn Espisito, Nick's attorney, was also present that day for the civil proceedings against his ex's father, allowing him finally to begin the process of rebuilding his life.

Part of the rebuilding process included me. The bond between us was too great, and it wasn't long before we were drawn back to each other, those intense feelings we'd had for each other never subsiding. During my time in DC, he'd actually flown up from Texas to escort us home. He supported the Children's Justice Foundation, helping me coordinate fundraisers, and attending events with me whenever he could. As always he continued to show his true blue colors as both a person and a man, and his thoughtful and caring actions continued to remind my heart that there were good people out in the cold, lonely world.

I knew I didn't want to live without him, and we began to make plans for the future. Whatever uncertainty or challenges lay ahead, we decided we would face them together, and work on building the foundation that would allow us to do that. I was happily surprised when Chad proposed to me, and I accepted without hesitation. I couldn't have been happier to have this wonderful man by my side, and I admit I never thought I would love or be loved again. Like so many women who experience heartbreak and turmoil at the hands of the man you love, you begin to embrace the notion that you'll never love again. You think yourself unworthy and undeserving of love, and you close your heart away from the possibility of ever finding your soul mate.

I had believed what I had with Nick was a true and lasting love. With Chad in my life, I've been shown what it is like to be in a happy and healthy relationship with a partner who truly loves and respects you. When in a relationship, a man is supposed to PROFESS, PROTECT, and PROVIDE for his woman; Chad practices all three with me each and every day. I never have to wonder where I stand with him, or what his feelings are for me. He shows me every day through his words and actions just how deep his devotion is to me, to our family, and to his faith. His love was worth waiting for. I can now see so clearly that what Nick and I engaged in was far from a loving relationship, but rather a sick attachment built on fear, ego, and intense physical attraction. After Nick's constant betrayals, I certainly believed I would never find true love again, and had closed off that part of my life. However, God works in mysterious ways, and he brought Chad to me to show me that love wasn't through with me yet, and that indeed it was possible for me to find my one true love. Chad and I are connected in a way that I've never experienced before. Oftentimes, he can just look at me and know exactly what I'm thinking or feeling. He takes care of my emotional needs like no one ever has. Whenever I'm in the doldrums, he always brings me out of them. He is the man I always dreamed of and needed, the one I kept looking for in all the wrong places. There have never been any whispers with Chad, only peace, harmony, and love.

As part of our pledge to each other, Chad and I decided we needed a fresh start. I was still with my parents, and devoting much of my time to fending off legal salvos and building my foundation. However, it was time for me to elevate myself to the next level of my life and use every resource at my disposal to get my kids back. Marrying Chad and building a life with him would certainly provide the stability I needed and wanted, and would absolutely provide the family structure I'd been searching for my entire life. Kaytlin, whose own father has shunned her, spending almost no time with her, loved Chad and called him Dad. Chad and Kylan, who is eighteen now, got along so well that we decided he would come and live with us on a full-time basis. My long-held dream of having a traditional family would finally be coming true, even if two pieces were missing.

Chad and I knew the only way we could begin anew in

earnest would be to leave Texas. While Texas was home for both of us, and where our families were, it held bitter memories for us both. I was constantly reminded that the laws of Texas had conspired against me to take my children away and allowed repeated offenses against the people closest to me. Texas was where Nick and Tommy had stalked and abused me, and in general had made my life a living hell. Chad is Creek Indian; his family resides in Oklahoma, and so that is where we decided to build our new family unit, and in the process tap into my lineage, which I believed would help me get my kids back once and for all.

On my father's side of the family I am a descendent of the Cherokee/Choctaw Indian tribe. I am one quarter Cherokee/Choctaw, making my children one eighth, which was just enough to get them to be considered Native American. As such we would fall under the protection, and more importantly the jurisdiction/sovereign nation, of the Indian government. In the United States, the laws of Native American tribes trump all state law (due to the Indian Child Welfare Act). Moving under their protection meant I would receive free legal representation, and would be allowed to present my evidence in an unbiased courtroom to an unbiased judge. I filed for an address confidentiality program so neither Nick nor his family, or any of the other unscrupulous attorney or officials, would be able to find me with the evidence I had. It was approved within twenty-four hours by the State of Oklahoma. I could finally be granted my long sought-after protective orders. I am getting my kids back.

Sometimes in life it is necessary to take a step back and figure out where we've gone wrong in order to figure out how to go right. That means transforming our mindset and taking a new path. I lived in Texas pretty much my whole life, and it was all I knew. However, I was able to take a moment to realize that staying there wasn't in my best interest, or in the best interest of my children. I knew in the long run I would need to make that sacrifice in order to fulfill the promise of a brighter future for myself and for my children.

I could—and have—shed many tears about the loss of my children and how we were ripped apart. However, I recognized that feeling sorry for myself and curling up in a ball wouldn't do any of us any good. I would not live that way. I would take the proactive path, and engage in positive actions. I would believe, achieve, and receive. These are the principles I chose to apply to my life. If I held onto the belief that I would get my kids back, I would. I knew it would be a hard journey—it's already been a hard journey. But nothing in life is worth having if we don't fight for it with everything we have.

I've been knocked down, dragged through the mud, stalked, terrorized, choked, and spit on. I've been lied to, lied about, and been caught in a web of deceit so twisted and tangled it seemed I would never be free. I've seen the highest of highs, and the lowest of lows. I've seen the pure joy that exists in people, and the darkness of evil glittering in the eyes of far too many. I've been through it all, and yet somehow I'm still able to live my life as the gift that it is. thankful for drawing breath, thankful for all four of my beautiful children, and ready for another chance to stand for what is right—thankful that I get another day to emerge victorious.

When I ask myself now, "How did I get here?" I know exactly how. I let those around me determine the course of my destiny, rather than taking the reins of my life in my own two hands to propel the horse forward down the trail. I put on blinders against the lies and treachery, and allowed myself to be manipulated. I shut my ears against the deafening whispers telling me to heed what I knew to be true in my heart.

But no more. For the first time in my life, I am a whole person, and one who I love with all my flaws and quirks. I accept me for me and no longer need validation from anyone else to justify all that is wonderful about me. Once I was able to make that realization, true and lasting love blossomed in my life. The flickers of hope for getting my children back burn brighter than ever, and I know this time they WILL come home to me. My faith has sustained me and helped to push me forward to bigger and better things. I have become a vessel of hope for others. My passion and purpose have been realized—that children are the greatest assets; they are our future. I know it is better to build up a child than to repair an adult. My children and the children of the world are most vital, and worth fighting for in order to reform the system and stop allowing the emotional abuse of children.

I will never be victimized again, because I have learned the lessons and heeded the advice, and grown from it.

I am standing strong.

About the Author

Jennie Morton graduated summa cum laude with honors, earned a bachelor of science degree in psychology/business, and was accepted into South Texas College of Law in 2003. She is the founder and president of the Children's Justice Foundation, which works to spread awareness of how children can be abused by the legal system. Jennie lives in Oklahoma and has four children—Kylan, Kaytlin, Aidan, and Hunter.

Support the Children's Justice Foundation

Children's Justice Foundation provides educational programs designed to improve understanding of how divorce, custody, and other high-conflict legal matters can impact children. We are offering these educational programs to both parents to children in these situations as well as attorneys, judges, and other legal affiliates.

For more information e-mail:
childrensjusticefoundation@yahoo.com